THE PRODUCTIVE
LEADER

How to Achieve More, Reduce Stress and Gain 2 Hours Per Day

SALLY FOLEY-LEWIS

"In the future of work where having influence relies on self-leadership, delegation and high performance, those who are productive leaders will be the ones who thrive. Productive leadership is the number-one skill for every current and aspiring business leader to have in their tool belt. Sally's insights in this book are powerful and command attention. Two words: read it!"
– Jane Anderson, Influence Expert

"What I love about Sally is her honesty. She genuinely and deeply understands the real challenges of leadership and organisation, and her insights go far beyond the prosaic to the powerful. She also understands our inherent resistance to change, and the criticism and rejection that people living in their power often experience from those who want to stay victims. If you are among the people who claim sovereignty over their own lives – and you want to help others do the same – you need to read this book to gain the strategies and systems Sally shares. And book her to speak to your teams. She's good."
– Catherine Palin-Brinkworth M.AppSci CSP, Founder – Progress Performance International

"I've just finished reading *The Productive Leader* and I've finally figured out where I've been going wrong all these years! As a lifelong learner, I'm always willing to review how I do things with a view to improving my work habits and lifestyle. I love this book,

jam-packed with well-thought-out concepts that are easy to implement and the best part: they work! Nice work, Sally."
– Lindsay Adams CSP, Global Speaking Fellow, The Relationships Guy

"I've always been in awe of Sally's processes, lists, plans, posters, journals, etc. She knows how to get things done, and she gets on with it. Now I know this 'bossy and organised' trait is something she's had since childhood. All I can say is – it works! With so many distractions today, longer-than-ever to-do lists and stress on the rise, we could all do with some help. Sally breaks down her expertise and processes into an easy-to-read format. If we all followed her advice, there would be a lot more productive leaders around!"
– Shirley Taylor, International Author of Model Business Letters, Emails & Other Business Documents 7th Edition, and CEO, STTS Training Pty Ltd, Singapore

"Sally Foley-Lewis has written the penultimate book on productivity! Cleverly crafted with real-world strategies that you can implement in a matter of minutes, it will be become an all-time classic reference book for the modern leaders of business. Well done … 10 out of 10!"
– Keith Abraham CSP, Multi-Award-Winning Keynote Speaker, 5 x Best-selling Author, Founder of the Passionate Performance Program

"Sally Foley-Lewis is the real deal. She practices what she shares in this book. She shares not only what works for her clients, but what she puts into practice to make her one of the most productive people I know. Her book is filled with practical ideas shared clearly and with humour. Your small investment in this productivity tool will pay off many times over – if you apply her techniques to your life."
– Rebecca Morgan, CSP, CMC, Best-selling Author of 26 books, USA

"What I share with my clients is that as a leader, you need to achieve more by doing less. Sally's book strongly reflects that principle. Productivity is so much more than time management. It is about leveraging your resources to achieve your highly focused goals and Sally's work embodies this. I am thrilled that Sally has been able to capture her work on the written page. As an absolute dynamo, it was only a matter of prioritisation to make it happen. As a speaker and a coach, she has enabled her clients to achieve fantastic results. The ideas she has shared in this book will boost her to the next level. Congratulations, Sally, on a book that is essential for every leader and potential leader to read and incorporate into their everyday habits."
– Warwick Merry CSP, Master MC, Success Speaker and 2017 National President Professional Speakers Australia

"What if you could read a book and get back two hours in every workday? That is a reality when you read Sally Foley-Lewis's excellent book, *The Productive Leader*. Sally teaches you how to work smarter and calmer, which beats working harder every day of the week! Highly recommended."
– Cathy Fyock, Author, Speaker, Book Coach, USA

"Technology was supposed to make us more productive. But like building a house, unless you have a solid foundation, it doesn't matter what program, app or plug-in you use, you are unlikely to achieve long-term, sustainable results. In a world full of information and 'noise', *The Productive Leader* cuts through the 'fluff' and shines a light on the fact that if you don't get the foundation right, nothing else matters."
– Donna Hanson, Certified Speaking Professional, Productivity with Technology Specialist

"Sally has written a book that is extremely readable, packed with case studies and examples. Gone are the days when productivity equated solely to time management. Sally shares how productivity is about 'focusing on the effectiveness of your efforts'. She offers practical tools to change our behaviours so we can increase our personal productivity and the productivity of the people we lead. If you also want to be a productive leader, then this is the book for you."
– Mel Kettle, Communication and Social Media Expert

"In this phenomenal book, Sally Foley-Lewis says, 'It matters not what role you're in or what your job title is. You are a leader. A leader is not a job title – it's a behaviour.' This gem alone can transform the path of a human being. Sally is one of those people whose insights are powerful and command attention. Read. This. Book!"
– **Karen Jacobsen, The GPS Girl**

"Who has time to be more productive? I'm too busy! Feel lighter, less stress and learn to become more accountable for results with *The Productive Leader* by Sally Foley-Lewis."
– **Scott Friedman CSP, Global Speaking Fellow, Founder of Together We Can Change the World**

"I have been waiting for this book to be released. *The Productive Leader*. It says it all, really: we all want to be just that in our lives. Step by step, Sally takes us through just how to achieve that and so much more. From the moment I met Sally, the one thing that struck me, apart from her intelligence, was her passion for helping people and companies to have a happier and healthier workplace. She has a very clear vision on how she can help give back the valuable time we would all love more of. Her passion, leadership and brilliant organisational skills now make so much sense to me since reading her book. She has been passionate about organising the best for herself and those around her since she was a child. If you

have a small business, a large company, are the CEO of a company, the head of a department or are time poor in even running your own life, I highly recommend you grab your copy and read it carefully. You will learn so much on how to become more effective in your daily life, all while getting back some precious time to spend exactly how you want to. As Sally says, you can work harder, or smarter and calmer. I know what I choose. Sally, on a personal note I wish you every success with your book. You are one of the most caring, funny, authentic, real and smart women I know who deserves all the success in the world."
– Tracey Mathers, Managing Director, Tracey Mathers Pty Ltd

"Sally's capacity to unpack, explain and advise on how to be a more productive leader is captured in these pages."
– David Penglase CSP, Intentionomics

"Loved your insights and the way they were delivered with a combination of storytelling and statistics. I could see myself in your examples, and what I can see I can take action on. Productivity has increased and time has been saved. Thank you!"
– Julie Cross CSP

"Sally is one of those people whose insights are powerful and command attention. She has shifted my thinking. The result? I've found another hour in most

days to focus on income-producing activities and created an extra 30% sales in only two months. What a return on the investment! Read this book!"
– Ian Stephens CSP, Author of *The 7 Universal Laws of Sales Success*, Founder of enRIch Training & Development

(CSP = Certified Speaking Professional, the highest accreditation level for the professional speaking industry worldwide.)

For Mum,
the most productive leader I know!

ABOUT THE AUTHOR

Sally Foley-Lewis has spent the past 20 years coaching and mentoring people to become more productive. She develops leaders' efficiency by building their people and team skills, improving their task management and nurturing their self-leadership. She works with middle managers and team leaders in large corporates and associations in Australia and overseas, as well as employers in small to medium-sized businesses.

Essentially, she is a productivity and leadership expert. Obsessed with execution, Sally enables people to not only get on with their work, but with their peers, senior leaders and teams. The flow-on effect of this is profound: leaders witness an even greater level of engagement and productivity from their team members.

What makes Sally different to other coaches is that she, too, has been a manager and CEO. She knows first-hand the pressure of balancing your own workload, leading a team and delivering the required outcomes. Sally has experienced the struggle of life in the trenches, so she truly gets it!

Sally has also trained and developed managers and leaders across a diverse range of industries in Australia and overseas. Her unique skillset and depth of experience means she knows how to make real, lasting improvements to productivity. It's more than a mere concept of time or people management. It's a journey.

As a leader, it's easy to identify the tasks you should be delegating. The challenge is knowing how to delegate these tasks and who to. Working with different people means managing, influencing and manoeuvring different personalities. You may be avoiding certain conversations that deep down you know should have, but you're not sure how to start or you're afraid of the ramifications. If you look at your week ahead it overwhelms rather than excites you, it can impact the way you lead your team. It can also impact how effective you are at achieving what's required. Your home life can be affected, too.

Sally understands this. She can help you begin the conversations you need to have so you can move forward. She can help you work through your fears, take control of your leadership and be excited about your work again.

Sally speaks, mentors, trains and coaches PRODUC-TIVITY and LEADERSHIP. She does this through workshops, presentations and mentoring for leaders who want to build their skills and confidence so they can lead their teams more effectively – by delegating appropriately, leading difficult conversations with confidence, and giving feedback in ways that effect positive change.

Sally can help you understand the different team roles and behaviours at play and why conflicts arise. More importantly, she teaches you how to resolve them quickly.

One key change Sally helps leaders make is eliminating that constant, heavy feeling of telling and retelling and getting nowhere. You *can* feel lighter, more productive and less stressed. Sally will show you that through delegating, coaching and setting accountability, you can become an empowered, more productive leader.

To find out more about Sally and her programs, go to www.sallyfoleylewis.com

ACKNOWLEDGEMENTS

Ask for help. Not because you are weak.
But because you want to remain strong.
– Les Brown

Distilling the experience, learning and thinking about *The Productive Leader* would not have been possible without the wisdom, guidance and support of many people.

While the notion of *The Productive Leader* only came to me recently, it has been slowly bubbling away for my entire life. As such, I must thank my early influencers – my family and my teachers. I want to thank Alan Nolan, an amazing teacher who empowered a class of 10- and 11-year-olds to step up and take responsibility: that overnight camp taught me about going for what I want, speaking up, working as a team, and what a sense of achievement feels like. Thank you also to Alkoomi, my Girl Guides leader, who saw so much potential in her patrol leaders and had that right blend of magic and wisdom that empowered us to shine and achieve.

To my professional family who never settle and don't

let anyone deliver less than their best. I owe so much to so many. I do want to say a special thank you to Jane Anderson, Jennifer Leone and Joanna Thumiger.

To the Thought Leaders Business School for giving me a phenomenally more thorough, elegant and unique way of thinking and sharing my experience and knowledge – thank you. The journey to thought leadership is just that, a journey. I will strive to continuously think deeper, challenge assumptions and be worthy of being part of the tribe.

To the clients I work with every day, your tenacity to be better and more powerful productive leaders is inspirational. To see and play a small part in the impact your leadership journey has on the people you lead and serve because you do the work on yourself, your task management and your people skills fills me with gratitude.

To Martin, who constantly shows me the value of deep thinking and demonstrates his love and devotion in patience and in deed. Thank you. Thank you for being you and encouraging me to be my best. I love you.

To the editing and publishing team, Lauren Shay of Full Stop Writing, Editing and Design and Sylvie Blair of BookPOD, your expertise means I can share my ideas productively! Thank you.

CONTENTS

CONTENTS

SALLY FOLEY-LEWIS

INTRODUCTION

As a young girl, before I started school, I remember playing with an old typewriter. I wasn't old enough to know how to spell many words, but I knew that a typewriter produced documents of words. I would tap away on those keys pretending I was typing the most important reports, memos and letters. With head held high and chest puffed with pride, I would pull pages out of the typewriter with gusto and stack the sheets neatly on the corner of my makeshift desk. I would then boldly walk – most likely stomp – around the front room (AKA my office), giving all my imaginary minions tasks to do. I was in my little happy place with order and a hint of bossiness.

If you asked my mum what's one thing she remembers about me when I was in primary school, she would tell you how bossy and organised I was. Mum loves to share the story of how I was one of the key instigators of the students' demand that my primary school provide softer, better-quality toilet paper. I don't recall much of the situation, but I, along with my comrades, organised a petition. Did we get softer, better toilet paper? I honestly can't remember. Being organised, wanting to improve a situation and being a bit bossy – that I do remember!

I aspired to work in a position of leadership. Back then, I thought to have a job title that included words such as chief, executive or manager meant I was the best, that I had made it! So, when I became the head of a youth organisation, my ego well and truly went into overdrive. I really thought I had made it.

That lasted all of a week – if that! I quickly discovered how challenging it was to go from working with my colleagues to being their "boss"; to manage multiple and shifting priorities; to make sense of, filter and translate broad strategic information (that changed so much and often your head would spin) into operational language; oh, and to grow the membership.

It was lonely and it impacted my life professionally and personally. I had to stop and re-think my approach to the way I worked, the way I led my team, and the way I led myself.

I had two saving graces. The first was the dedication of the team I had the privilege of working with. Was it all sweetness and roses? No, of course not. But overall, they were a great team. The second was the ultimatum I was given at home: it was a "something's gotta give" situation. It was the toughest and best wake-up call I had ever received!

My involvement with youth leadership and service organisations as I grew up (even working for a few) and learning first-hand the role of the leader prompted me to blend my inner organiser with my love of service. This mix is no doubt a fundamental influence on my obsession with helping leaders be more productive. I don't want any leader to feel what I felt or to go through what I went through. This is why I share my stories, learning and insights.

Today, I work with dedicated professionals who know that leadership is a behaviour. It's a journey, and part of being a successful leader is constantly looking for ways to improve. Being a productive leader encompasses all this. I have the great privilege of working with thousands of managers across multiple industries, internationally and in Australia. I'm passionate about helping them to be successful leaders. No matter the geography or the culture, common productivity challenges face us all. No one can escape the reach of productivity.

I'm excited to share this book with you. It matters not what role you're in or what your job title is. *You are a leader.* A leader is not a job title – it's a behaviour. If you have a burning desire to be a better, happier and more productive leader in your life and for your team, business or organisation, then this book is for you.

When leaders are more productive, they confidently and consistently achieve top results. They are engaged and engaging. They are, quite simply, happier.

INTRODUCTION

This book is for you if you know there's got to be a better way, but you're struggling to find it. This book is for you if you feel control slipping away. It's for you if you want to achieve more, reduce stress and gain two hours per day.

Enjoy.

PRODUCTIVITY IS NEVER AN
ACCIDENT. IT IS ALWAYS THE
RESULT OF A COMMITMENT
TO EXCELLENCE, INTELLIGENT
PLANNING AND FOCUSED
EFFORT.

– PAUL J. MEYER

SALLY FOLEY-LEWIS

CHAPTER 1

PRODUCTIVITY: IT'S NEVER JUST BEEN ABOUT TIME MANAGEMENT

Time management is a misnomer! Productivity is about focus – focusing on the effectiveness of your efforts.

When you mismanage your effort and energy, that is, when you:

- Miss deadlines
- Delay decision making that affects others
- Start projects late
- Procrastinate
- Ignore agendas
- Take risky short cuts without considering consequences to quality, success and stakeholders
- Speed through tasks without checking accuracy and quality, which leads to re-doing work
- Delay submitting work because it's not perfect …

… it not only costs you and the organisation money, it makes you look unprofessional and it negatively impacts others.

It also gives decision makers cause for concern when considering whether you deserve a bonus, pay rise or promotion.

In an article by BaseX, referring to its own research, the cost of poor productivity was calculated to be $US650 billion per annum in the US. Research commissioned by Medibank (one of Australia's health insurers) in 2005 found that presenteeism alone costs $A25.7 billion annually. Presenteeism, in simple terms, is being at work while sick.

When I think of the term *time management*, I envisage a stressed clock watcher: someone who is forever looking at and obsessing with the time, rather than focusing on the work they're meant to be doing and the quality of that work.

Consider Percy Whiting's quote:

> *"Time is a fixed income, and as with any income, the real problem facing us is how to work successfully with our daily allotment. Plan each day down to the moment because once time is wasted, you can never get it back."*

To my way of thinking, Whiting is asking us to be vigilant with how we spend our time. We must plan it and use it wisely, rather than merely watch the clock.

According to the Australian Bureau of Statistics (ABS, 2010), managers work longer hours per week than any other occupational group, with the average manager working 43.3 hours per week. I suspect that is quite a conservative number. If you are averaging 43.3 hours per week or more, then something needs to change!

You can achieve more in the time you have with a lot less stress when you pay attention to your productivity. It's not only your personal productivity. It's also your professional productivity, the way in which you get your work done, and the way in which you help your team get their work done. It's your interactions with other people. All these factor into improving productivity. Ignoring one element will cause an imbalance in your day-to-day life. You might be able to cope with and sustain that imbalance in the short term, but in the long-term, problems will crop up. And those problems can be costly.

To give you a picture of what this might look like, consider these two real scenarios:

In the short term, you might be able to work a few extra hours per week. But in the long term, you will become exhausted, miss out on life events, and your physical and mental health may suffer.

You might be able to ignore some minor conflict going on between two of your team members because they "should" be able to work it out. In the short term, this might not seem too serious. However, if the conflict isn't resolved, it may escalate into something toxic, resulting in bullying claims, stress leave, turnover … it all adds up and can cost you and the business dearly.

CHALLENGES THAT IMPACT PRODUCTIVITY

So, what happens to us? Why do we have problems with our productivity? Here are some common challenges and fears that leaders face.

CHALLENGES:

- **Shifting Priorities**
  Change is the only constant in our world today. Leaders sometimes struggle to be agile enough to adapt at the right pace and in the right direction. They also need to bring their teams along, so the ability to influence and guide people through fast change is vital.

- **Driving Performance**
  Achieving more and better results with a leaner workforce means leaders must be able to drive performance effectively while keeping turnover levels low. They also must keep the workforce en-

gaged, develop individuals in line with new technologies and processes, and maintain a high-performing and functioning team.

- **A New Generation**
  With baby boomers retiring, so too does their experience. This means that organisations are losing cost-effective, reliable on-the-job training and in-house mentors. The challenge for leaders is to find new ways to rapidly equip younger leaders with the necessary skills and knowledge to productively lead.

- **Emails, Emails, Emails!**
  Inboxes are clogged with emails demanding attention. Leaders struggle with inbox and task management while dealing with other jobs and projects appropriately and in a timely manner. The overwhelm of email won't stop. By 2019, we'll receive, on average, 260 emails per day with at least 75% of those emails requiring specific action. So, it's crucial that leaders find a way to manage their inboxes without overwhelm, and to help their teams to productively handle their own emails.

- **Communication and Culture**
  Fundamentally, the key to a productive workforce is how individuals communicate through and across the organisation. Communication sig-

nificantly impacts the culture of the organisation, which in turn impacts productivity. Leaders must ensure effective, open and respectful communication. Refereeing, fire-fighting and getting caught up in interpersonal conflicts distract everyone from getting their work done.

- **Long Hours and Missed Moments**
  In this constantly connected world, accessing emails and texts and taking calls at all hours of the night, day and weekend leaves leaders and their workforce exhausted. Keep in mind the ABS's finding that managers work longer hours in a week compared to any other workforce category. Staying at work late and bringing work home leads to tired leaders who take longer to complete tasks. This means leaders can be less present for family and personal pursuits.

WHAT KEEPS LEADERS AWAKE AT NIGHT

- **Failure**
  With the pressure to get more done with better results – and often with less resources – leaders do not want to be perceived as failures. Their need for success, through the team they lead and the outcomes they achieve, is often driven by high expectations and standards that can stifle and inadvertently hinder productivity.

- **Ownership**

  Leaders can be consumed with the fear that they aren't making the right decisions. They agonise over whether they are driving team performance the "right" way and can hold back from speaking up for fear of saying the wrong thing. This results in a lack of ownership of their leadership role.

- **Backlash and Bullies**

  Leaders often avoid difficult conversations because they fear they'll be called a bully. The real and perceived ramifications of this label become too high. The stress of avoidance impacts the whole team, which makes the leader even more ineffectual.

- **Contributing**

  Leaders may decide against speaking up or contributing in key meetings for fear it will reflect on them poorly. They may also be concerned that they'll be challenged by others. Their fear of not having all the answers means they fail to meaningfully contribute.

- **Imposter Syndrome**

  Leaders often wonder if they are truly cut out for their role. They question whether they are good enough to be an effective and productive leader. This is known as "imposter syndrome". If not dealt with, imposter syndrome can impede the success of anyone, especially leaders who question or doubt the validity of how they got a leadership role in the first place.

- **Being Good Enough**
  Being a good provider for the family often drives people into higher management or leadership roles, despite personal career desires. This can lead to the wrong person being in the wrong role.

How often do you wish you had more hours in the day? How often do you hear your team members say they want more time to get their work done? *"If only I had an extra hour every day."* You know that's not possible, yet it's so common to hear. Thinking about it doesn't help. Stressing about it is even worse, and unhealthy. It's a waste of energy.

With these challenges and fears, it's understandable that productivity is impacted. It makes sense that you think pushing hard will make you more productive. "I just have to work harder," we often tell ourselves. But do you stop to think about whether it's the right kind of push? Is it helping or hindering productivity? Have you ever done something you thought was going to have a great outcome, only to find it blow up in your face? You can be working long hours and working hard, but feel as though you're getting nowhere.

It's clichéd, but it's true: you can work harder or smarter! I've put my own little twist on that: you can work harder or work smarter *and* calmer!

To make sense of why your productivity may not be where it should be, refer to the Productive Leadership Model:

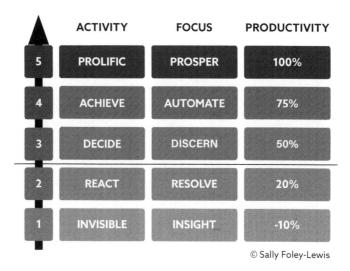

© Sally Foley-Lewis

The Productive Leadership Model.

Read through the level descriptions. At what level do you see yourself?

LEVEL ONE: INVISIBLE > INSIGHT

One step forward, two steps back!

At this lowest level, the activity you're engaged in feels virtually invisible. It's not that you're not doing anything, it's just that it's not seen by others, or not enough of it is seen. Its impact fails to progress your productivity. Everything you do seems invisible in the eyes of everyone around you, especially those you want to be seeing you.

It feels as though you're taking one step forward and two steps back. It's not good for your confidence. Instead of giving you a sense of achievement, it gives you a sense of chasing your tail. It's busier than busy. It's not being lazy – it's simply being ineffectual. You're not getting the results you deserve.

To shift up from this level, you need greater insight. With that insight, you can stop doing the "wrong" things and start doing the "right" things. You can start thinking about the sequence of activities you're doing. Insight is essential for working out what to stop, start, change or continue. It's self-awareness. It's conducting a self-audit. It might be tough to face the reality of the situation, but it's truly liberating to let go of what's not working.

LEVEL TWO: REACT > RESOLVE

You're a fire-fighter – all you can do is react to the noise and sirens.

Every minute of every day is spent in reaction. At this level, you are a fire-fighter. You constantly respond to calls and put out fires. Rarely do you get the chance to catch your breath and get on top of your workload. You might end each day saying something like, "It must have been a good day – no one died."

Everything you do amounts to only just covering yourself and your team. When something lands on your desk, you react and act immediately. You may not feel as though you're behind with your work, but you certainly don't feel that you're ahead of the game.

You must acknowledge that some tasks or projects have to go. Ask yourself, "What am I doing that results in me only ever reacting? What am I doing that stops me from being proactive?" You need to understand that not everything can happen at once. Sequences and the ability to prioritise are required.

At this level, it's common to say "yes" most of the time and "no" only some of the time. Because you feel the pressure to say yes to everything, you give the impression that you lack clarity. You lack the confidence to stick with what you know is right. You feel obliged to say yes because you can see the merit in everything.

LEVEL THREE: DECIDE > DISCERN

You've got brand-new glasses to see more clearly.

You're above the line and making progress. At this level, you make quality decisions and have learnt to say no to the tasks, ideas and projects that don't merit immediate attention. Prioritising is starting to pay off for you. You might still get excited by some ideas and tasks. You might even be afflicted with "shiny new object syndrome", where something comes across your path and you think, "Oh, this would be such a great activity for the team to get into." However, it doesn't serve your purpose or it doesn't get decided upon without some level of discernment, such as, "Will this add to or dilute what we're here to do?"

This is not about saying no to everything. It's about being discerning. It's more than okay to get excited about a new initiative or project. But make sure it's helping rather than hindering. If it hinders, it will cost time, productivity and money, without the return.

At this level, you become a better and more confident decision maker. You are learning what factors are most important in ensuring your decisions are productive for you, your work and your team. It also means helping the team become more discerning about the way they work so they can be more productive.

Once you are more discerning, you are a role model for your team. You empower and teach your team to be discerning as well, and their productivity increases.

LEVEL FOUR: ACHIEVE > AUTOMATE

It's like trying to put the hose back onto the tap while the water is still running at full pressure.

You are achieving a great deal. You often feel as though you are on top of your workload and the team is functioning well. You have far more wins than you have losses, but you are still working harder rather than smarter or calmer.

It's time to re-evaluate your work and determine what can be automated, outsourced or delegated. It's the difference between knowing versus actually turning the tap off first, then re-attaching the hose. You've brought your team along this journey, so they too will be ready for you to delegate more. At this level, you are looking for ways to systemise processes and involve the team in creating standards and processes that can be easily handled by anyone in the team. You are delegating full projects or parts of projects to the high potentials in your team, freeing up your time to be a more strategic leader.

LEVEL FIVE: PROLIFIC > PROSPER

It's like a gentle, cool breeze sweeps over you on a hot, sunny day.

At this highest level, you've got insight, resolution, discernment, delegation and automation to back you. This means you're better placed to say yes to the right ideas, projects and opportunities. You are being prolific for your organisation or business. There's a sense of space in your day and there's capacity in your day, which gives you the opportunity to investigate how you can add more value to help yourself, your team and your department or organisation prosper.

So, where do you see yourself in the Productive Leadership Model?

Most leaders say they fluctuate between just above or below the line, between two and three. Some say they have *happy moments* at level four, but they're not permanent. It's important to understand where you sit in this model right now, because it can help you work out and sequence the action steps you need to take to move up and become more productive. It will enable you to *sustain* a productive approach to your leadership.

Levels one and two require leaders to focus on personal productivity. As you work up the levels, you focus more on task or professional productivity and people productivity. This makes sense in so many ways. If you've ever caught an aeroplane, you know that the safety announcement always demands that in case of an emergency, you must put your oxygen mask on first. You already know why: you must look after yourself before you can look after anyone else. The same concept applies to the productive leader. Get your oxygen mask – your personal productivity – in order first.

I have an oxygen mask hanging over my desk to constantly remind me of this very concept.

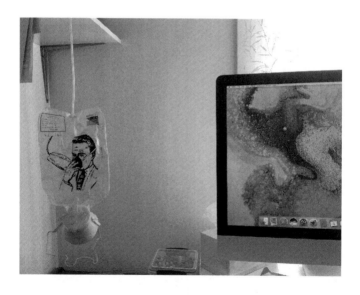

No matter where you currently sit in the Productive Leadership Model, the goal is to strive for level five: prolific. Being trapped in the lower levels is a lot like being trapped in a maze. It's a struggle to find your way out. And the lower you are, the more trapped you feel: just when you think you're out, something comes up and you get diverted to another direction. Just when you think you are on the right path, something changes. You chase your tail and nothing you do seems to make an impact. You're not lazy, you're exhausted, and you (and your family) can feel the pressure mounting. Your personal productivity and your approach to how you do your work and people productivity need an overhaul.

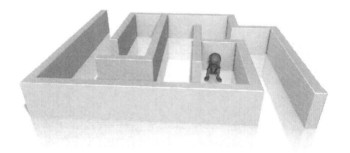

Conversely, when you have a plan, when you take action and move up to the higher levels so your focus and activity match your boosted productivity, it feels as though you're escaping the maze and jumping into a convertible! You're zooming along an open motor-way, the top's down, the wind's in your hair, the sun kisses your face and you feel as light as air. You're on top of the world. You are super achieving.

That's what this book, *The Productive Leader*, is all about. The aim is to get you unstuck and out of the maze so you can move from being invisible with your productivity to being prolific. You *can* gain two more hours in your day. You *can* achieve more in the time you have – and with a lot *less* stress.

YOU DON'T NEED MORE
TIME IN YOUR DAY.
YOU NEED TO DECIDE.

– SETH GODIN

CHAPTER 2

THE CASE FOR THE PRODUCTIVE LEADER

WHY BE A PRODUCTIVE LEADER?

To say productivity is a popular topic is a drastic understatement. Try doing a Google search of the word *productivity*. You will receive more than 22 million hits! This topic is Googled constantly, yet business leaders have never felt more ineffective and disconnected. We're working harder, yet feeling more unproductive than ever.

In my coaching and mentoring sessions, I often hear my clients sigh, "Yes, I do need to get better at my time management."

What they really mean is:

- *"I don't know how to pull back, set boundaries and say no."*
- *"I actually do love the feeling of knowing I'm needed and this means I work longer and longer hours."*
- *"I need to climb the ladder in this corporation because my family is relying on my success."*

CHAPTER 2

We need to do more than simply say that we'll get better with our time management. We need to get to the heart of why our productivity is so out of whack and make real, lasting changes.

Research tells us that:

- Multi-tasking can decrease productivity by 40%.
  – *Journal of American Psychology, 2015*

- Australians spend half a day per week on Facebook. In 2016, we spent 12.5 hours per week on Facebook – an increase of four hours per week compared to 2015.
  – *Sensis Social Media Report, 2016*

- American companies lose $65 billion annually due to employee sleep deprivation.
  – *The American Academy of Sleep Medicine, 2011*

- Experiments found that people are 12% more productive when they are happy.
  – *University of Warwick, 2014*

- The average office worker in the UK is only productive for 2 hours and 53 minutes a day.
  – *Vouchercloud poll, 2016*

In other words, many of us are distracted, stressed and failing to manage our time effectively.

It's not all doom and gloom, though. When we are able to find more effective ways of being productive, we experience more success, more happiness and more profits:

- In one survey regarding happiness and productivity by the University of Warwick in 2014, **72% of respondents said happiness involved making progress towards goals, even if they never achieved them.**

- Furthermore, across a range of experiments, the same researchers could link happiness and productivity. In fact, individuals have approximately **12% greater productivity** than a control group.

- According to the 50 Best Places to Work 2016 report, by research institute Great Place to Work Australia, revenue per employee **increased from $388,473 to $402,047 – an increase of 3.38%.** The report said:

  "Generally, these companies are driven by a fundamental philosophy that creating a great workplace is the right thing to do, both for employees and business. It should be stressed, however, that there are definite business benefits: lower employee turnover, better applicant pool, greater product innovation, stronger client relationships, and better long-term growth. When it comes to the financial results, great work-

places deliver; maximising their opportunities to at-
tract and retain talent, and boost productivity while
minimising turnover."

• Furthermore, these top places to work recorded **89% employee engagement**, compared to Gallup's workforce poll, which showed 24% employee engagement.

This kind of research provides a convincing argument for boosting your productive leadership. It's evidence that the implementation of more effective practices can help drive task productivity and your team's performance. But productive leadership isn't about *doing* more. It's about *achieving* more. It's about engaging in procedures that don't rob you of time, effort, energy and joy. Productive leadership means achieving greater effectiveness for you and your team.

Before we look at *how* you can become a productive leader, you need to understand your *why*. Exactly why do you need to be more productive? What would it mean to you? To figure this out, ask yourself the following questions:

1. What would you do with two extra hours per day?
2. How are you getting in the way of your own productivity?
3. What areas of your leadership require a deeper level of self-awareness?

4. What extra value could you achieve by assessing the way you get work done?
5. Which relationships need greater focus for improved productivity?

Answer these questions thoughtfully and honestly. No doubt you will realise there are spaces, skills, insights and knowledge that could do with an overhaul. If so, then you have your "why". It's your reason for picking up this book.

One of my clients, Jason, was a business leader who was feeling overwhelmed. It had all become too much, so he gave me a call. The first thing we did was reflect on these five questions.

His answer to the first question – "What would you do with two extra hours per day?" – was the fundamental reason for why he needed to make changes. He wanted to spend more time with his family. He felt he was missing out and they were growing apart. He said that when he got home, usually late, he felt he was intruding. It was as though he was entering a stranger's family. Realising that was an incredibly powerful moment – one that shook Jason to his core. Because he was prepared to reflect on the questions, it meant he was ready to find ways to be a more productive leader so he could stop feeling like a stranger to his own family.

Take the time to reflect on the five questions. You will discover that you have your own motivations and reasons for why you must become a more productive leader. And if you'd like to share your answers with me, I'd be honoured. You can send them to me directly at sally@sallyfoleylewis.com.

THE THREE KEYS TO BEING THE PRODUCTIVE LEADER

The productive leader understands that there is more to productivity than meeting deadlines, coming in under budget and managing staff. The productive leader understands success comes when the three keys of productive leadership are connected and working in alignment.

The three keys are personal productivity, professional productivity and people productivity.

© Sally Foley-Lewis

The 3 Ps of Productivity.

1. PERSONAL PRODUCTIVITY

Being a productive leader starts with you: your personal productivity. Remember the oxygen mask: you need to put yours on before you can help anyone else. When you have effective personal productivity, the positives flow over into task and people productivity.

If you want your team to be more productive, first you need to do a self-audit. Take a good, hard look at your own behaviours, habits and routines. How do they impact your own productivity? Objectively and accurately answer the question, *"What am I doing to positively influence my sense of achievement, my ability to complete tasks effectively and the quality of the output I am achieving?"*

2. PROFESSIONAL PRODUCTIVITY

This productivity focuses on using the right tools and processes, backed by helpful habits, to get your work done: to be professional in your work! Not just any work, either: the right work in the right sequence. Professional productivity answers the question of how you can do your work in the most effective way possible.

3. PEOPLE PRODUCTIVITY

A successful productive leader empowers and engages their people. When the people in the organisation are productive, the results – be they financial, employee engagement or other – shine through. Helping your people find smarter and calmer ways to be productive is essential. Underlying that is the way they interact with each other. The productive leader keeps a keen eye on interpersonal communication through and across their team, department or organisation. The productive leader uses his or her personal and organisational authority carefully and respectfully to boost people productivity.

Personal, professional and people productivity form the three parts of this book. While each part could constitute a Master's degree in themselves, this book will equip you with the strategies you need. Best of all, they can be implemented immediately.

This book is the starting point – and by no means the end!

AT THE INTERSECTIONS

To make productive leadership sustainable, easier and more rewarding, it's important you pay attention to the intersections between the three Ps.

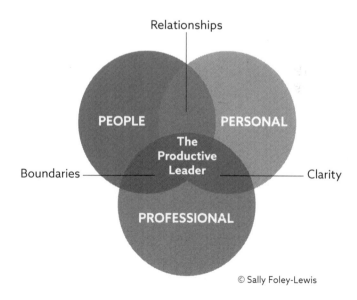

© Sally Foley-Lewis

Let's take a look at the three intersections:

1. At the intersection of personal productivity and professional productivity is **clarity**. This includes clear goal setting, understanding and establishing priorities, being able to review and revise priorities with a flexible mindset, and understanding the value and methods of the work being done so that productivity can be boosted.

2. At the intersection of professional productivity and people productivity are **boundaries**. This is where saying "no" and being an effective delegator are important. Influence and confidence in your role, and the expectations you have of yourself and others, form the boundaries that help teams and leaders get the work done.

3. At the intersection of people productivity and personal productivity are **relationships**. This is where the rubber hits the road. You need to have honest, respectful and open relationships because they positively influence the team, organisational productivity and results. No one is immune to the ramifications of a toxic organisational culture. The negative impact it has on productivity, results and outcomes can be immense. Relationships are the cornerstone of an organisation's culture, and that culture can either kill or nurture productivity.

The intersections of relationships, clarity and boundaries are critical to success. They must be factored into any efforts to improve productivity. We will explore them further over the next few pages, and the remainder of this book will provide you with strategies and tips for boosting your personal, professional and people productivity.

CLARITY

Without clarity, you wander aimlessly. Not only physically, but mentally, too. You plod along with no real direction. Clarity is about having clear goals, setting priorities, understanding the value of the work you're doing, and aligning your personal and professional values and goals.

There is a mammoth amount of research and data that demonstrates the high value of goal setting. The first empirical studies on goal setting as a way of team and self-achievement were conducted in the UK in the 1930s by industrial psychologist Cecil Alec Mace. He found that people with written goals were 50% more likely to achieve them than people who didn't write down their goals.

The giants of motivation, leadership, time management and productivity – Brian Tracy, Tony Robbins, Timothy Ferriss and Oprah, to name a few – have all talked about writing down their goals for greater clarity and improved, if not assured, chances of success. There is so much information available about the importance of goal setting for productivity, yet so few of us do it! There is a renowned goal-setting Harvard University alumni study that was conducted in 1979, then repeated in 1989. In 1979, graduates were asked if they had set clear written goals for their future: 84% had no specific goals, 13% had goals but they weren't written down, and 3% had clear, written goals and plans. In 1989, these same graduates were interviewed again. The 13% who had goals but had not written them down were earning twice as much as the 84% who didn't have any goals. Impressively, the 3% who had clear, written goals were earning on average 10 times as much as all the others!

While earning is one measure of success, the point to take from this is that clarity is critical for achieving goals and plans. Writing down goals and plans contributes to that clarity and boosts your commitment to achievement.

Clarity lies at the intersection of personal productivity and professional productivity:

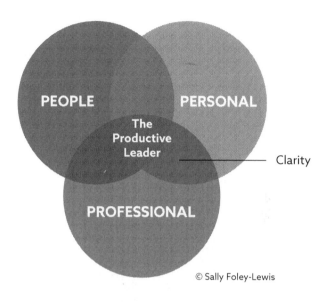

Clarity

© Sally Foley-Lewis

Clarity means you can be sure you are doing the right work, the right way, with the right resources and in the right time to achieve the right results. You have clarity when your goals, values and priorities work together, at times compromising yet without losing the big picture. These three key elements are aligned but agile enough so you can find ways to handle issues and challenges as they arise.

The Clarity Model helps leaders determine where they and their team members are in terms of having their goals, priorities and values aligned:

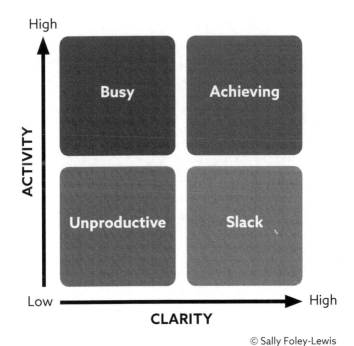

High

ACTIVITY

Low ➡ High

CLARITY

© Sally Foley-Lewis

The Clarity Model.

The **unproductive** quadrant is the most ineffective quadrant in the Clarity Model. There's low or no activity, and low or no clarity. It feels as though you're operating blind. The work you're doing is invisible. Operating in this quadrant means you are aimless.

When you have a high level of clarity but are low in activity, you are being **slack**. It's the "all talk and no action" quadrant. You know what to do, however you're choosing not to get the work done. It might be that you have a goal in mind, but you haven't written it down or you haven't set a plan to achieve it. Perhaps the goal doesn't align with your personal values, so you avoid doing the work.

On the top side of the model, where there is high activity but low clarity, you are **busy**: all work but no direction. You're like a chicken running around with its head cut off. You're reacting all the time and although you may have a goal, it's not a well-formed goal. Priorities may be missing, which leads you to do everything but the most valuable thing.

When you have a high level of activity that aligns with a high level of clarity, you're actually **achieving** (as opposed to just being busy). This is the quadrant to aim for. Operating from this quadrant gives you a feeling of execution and achievement. You might be busy, but you're not crazy-hectic busy. You're achieving. There's consistency and you're ticking off goals. You feel exhilarated because you can see your goals coming to fruition.

To truly have clarity as a productive leader, you must focus on:

- Goals
- Priorities
- Values

GOALS

The quickest way to move into the achieving quadrant is to write down a goal. The more specific you can be with your goal, the better your chances are of achieving it.

SMART goals have been around for a long time. In 1981, George T. Doran, Arthur Miller and James Cunningham wrote in a *Management Review* article, "There's a S.M.A.R.T. way to write management's goals and objectives."

SMART is an acronym for:

- Specific
- Measurable
- Achievable
- Realistic
- Time bound

Specific: The more specific your goals are, the more clarity you will have about the steps you need to take to achieve them.

Measurable: How will you measure your success? What will success look like when you've achieved your goal?

Achievable: Reaching a goal should involve some

challenge, but your goal shouldn't be so difficult that you'll never achieve it. When you can set your goal to be challenging yet achievable, you will avoid making it too easy and underwhelming!

Time bound: When will you achieve your goal? Working out a time frame for completing the necessary actions is critical. Too often, people underestimate this important element and say they'll reach their goal:

* By the end of July.
* Within one week.
* Before end of the year.

And my all-time favourite (*not!*):

* ASAP.

These timeframes are not specific enough. You will set yourself and your team up for failure with these loose deadlines. They might be clear in the mind of the person writing them, but they fail to consider the specific actions, communication and unforeseen work that must be done. Other issues may pop up and challenge the completion of the goal. Time bound means making a goal a top priority. It means determining a specific, non-negotiable date, such as 19th January, 2018, and even a time, such as 6pm.

Write your goals as SMART goals. Communicate them to your team and other relevant staff, including your senior leaders, to ensure they are achieved.

PRIORITIES

To achieve a goal, you need to prioritise. Know what needs to happen first and the sequence of actions. At times, your priorities may not be the same as the priorities of your organisation or others in your team. This is when compromise is needed to ensure there is a win-win for all involved.

A word of warning: know the difference between urgent and important. So often, "urgent" – usually what other people consider urgent – challenges what you've prioritised as important.

VALUES

What are your values? Do they align with the organisation's values? It's important to take a moment to reflect on this. Alignment is at the core of job satisfaction and productivity. Think about the organisation's goals, vision, mission and values. What stories can you tell to demonstrate that the organisation's values are evident in the work you do? Do these stories fill you with pride and leave you wanting more? Or do they conflict with your own values? The way these stories make you feel demonstrates whether your values are aligned with the organisation's or not. The more aligned they are, the more clarity there is. As such, this makes a positive contribution to productivity. Listen to the stories other people share about the work they do. They are values in action.

As you can see, clarity is a critical element of productivity success. Considering your goals, priorities and values, in what areas do you think you could do with a clarity boost?

TIPS TO BOOST CLARITY

1. If you have an exciting yet large goal ahead of you, break it down into smaller action steps so you don't get overwhelmed.

    Often when a big goal is created, it's written up as a SMART goal and that's where the action stops. The big SMART goal overwhelms you into procrastination because it's the big picture, the end that you have focused on, rather than the process.

    To move towards achieving the big goal, create short-term plans. For example, if your big goal is to be achieved within a timeframe of six months, then create monthly milestone plans. Following that, create weekly plans. Then add at least one action related to the weekly plan to your daily to-do list. Small actions lead to big transformations!

2. Once your team has goals and plans in action, talk about them at your regular staff meetings. Make them part of the normal language and culture in your workplace. Encourage everyone to openly discuss the goals and actions. Keep them alive and present amongst the team. Discuss and agree on how you can keep each other accountable. One of the best questions the productive leader can ask is: How would you like me to help you stay accountable?

3. Celebrate your achievements! Reinforce the positives of working hard and achieving goals by celebrating the successes. The productive leader acknowledges effort, persistence and results. Furthermore, they give support to their people who, not for the want of trying hard, didn't reach a goal. If a goal isn't reached, acknowledge the efforts and use it as a learning opportunity for the team.

BOUNDARIES

Boundaries enable you to say yes to the right opportunities and no to the potential pitfalls. They are rules you set for yourself and others to protect your values and your time.

Understanding and applying boundaries, no matter where you sit in the organisational chart, means you can be more productive. It ensures you do the right work, at the right time, to get the right results. Boundaries protect productivity. They protect time and effort because they ensure your focus is not encroached upon at the wrong time. They encourage the right behaviours and correct the wrong behaviours.

Burnout is a significant consequence of not having clear and enforced boundaries. Research by Kronos and Future Workplace (2017) shows that 32% of people say they have an unreasonable workload, and 32% say they do too much overtime or after-hours work. This can directly lead to burnout. It's an indication that they have no boundaries in place or that they are too loosely held.

It's not easy to say no. You may not realise that your boundaries are flimsy – or even too strict. It might be that you've never thought you could have boundaries. You may even think that setting boundaries could reflect badly on you. But this is not so: clear and reasonable boundaries show confidence. They let others know how to treat you and help you get your work done. They can also show your team, employees and colleagues how to deal with each other.

If someone asks you to do something and you can hear the voice in your head say, "I should say no," but you do it anyway, chances are your boundaries are too weak. If you say yes, then resent the fact you're doing the task, that, too, indicates a weak boundary.

When your boundaries are too weak and you (inadvertently) let people take advantage of you, it sends a message to others that they can do the same. You give them permission to take advantage.

For example, if colleagues, managers and friends let you get the coffee or make the tea each day, without ever offering to pay or make it themselves, then you're being taken for granted. Even if you say you're happy to do it, when will the gesture be repaid? Ask yourself: are your boundaries too weak? (Unless, of course, making or serving tea and coffee is your job, then I'll have a long black with milk, please!)

If you disclose some information about yourself, then feel anxious or vulnerable about what you've said, that is another indication of not having a clear boundary. The same fits if you share some information that makes others feel uncomfortable.

Conversely, sometimes your boundaries can be too strict. This may be the case if:

- You feel that no one knows or understands you.
- People describe you as someone who plays their cards close to their chest.
- You feel that you can't relate to others.
- You often dismiss or stop others' attempts to share things with you, such as a happy event, personal issue or even something work related.

- People stop calling you and inviting you to functions, even professional networking events.
- You enjoy the work you do, but it doesn't include anyone else.
- You feel disconnected, lonely or isolated.

If you've never worked on your boundaries before, you may feel uncomfortable at first. It's normal to feel a little resistance – from yourself and from others. Boundaries sit at the intersection of the work you do and the people you work with, so it makes sense that if you make changes to your boundaries, there'll be a period of adjustment for all involved.

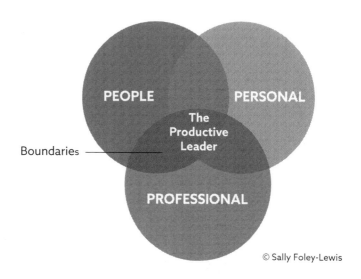

© Sally Foley-Lewis

It's important to have boundaries around behaviours, activities and tasks, as well as around your relationships at work and home. Boundaries are like fences around a house. Sometimes, the gates, garage, windows and doors are locked so no one can get in. You cut yourself off from everyone.

Other times, there's no fence and the front door is open. While this lets in some fresh air, it also allows others to pass through. When your boundaries are too open, people can take advantage and steal your belongings.

The saying that "fences make great neighbours" works well here. Boundaries are like fences and gates: you have control of them. It may not feel as though you do sometimes, but you do – and you need to. When you have boundaries in place, you are empowered. You have more control over your productivity.

Years ago, I worked for a training company. If I wasn't in the training room, I'd be at home designing and creating training materials. Although it was a part-time job, I worked full-time hours – at least – because I loved what I was doing.

One afternoon, my husband came to me and said, "Are you going to have a day off soon?" I replied, "What do you mean, I have time off all the time?" In my mind, I didn't work a nine-to-five job. Some days were long, some days were short. To me, I had breaks all the time, but my husband said, "You've been working 63 days straight."

Until that point, I hadn't realised. I'd let go of one of my boundaries. I felt guilty when I recognised that I hadn't had any time off with my husband. I had let the demand of the work and my enjoyment of the work creep in and take over other important parts of my life. Without realising it, I had allowed some of my values to be challenged.

To set your boundaries, you need to know your values. You must understand what's important to you and, therefore, what systems will support your boundaries and values. You need to communicate clearly what it is you will and won't do. Be explicit and tell people. Don't assume they can work it out from your behaviour.

Determine what is urgent and what is important for you and your productivity. You may also need to establish when and how you will step up and help other people with their urgent or important tasks.

Are you clear about the hours you work? Do you role model this to others? By working long hours day in, day out, you show that you have loose boundaries around your hours of work. You may also send a message to others that it's what's expected. But this way of working is not productive, healthy or sustainable.

In the same training company, our office manager got to a point where she turned her mobile phone off at

7pm because the managing director would call her at all hours – even as late as 10.30pm. Besides the fact she had a family, she was not paid to be on call 24/7. She informed the managing director of her boundary and told him she would not take calls after 7pm. To reinforce that boundary, she switched off her phone at 7pm. Did it backfire? Rarely. It was a clear and effective boundary that stopped the managing director from calling her at all hours.

Be okay with discussing your boundaries if someone crosses them. Talk about it straight away. If someone walked into your house without your permission, no doubt you'd have a few select things to say. You would address the matter immediately.

If someone does cross your boundaries, discuss it with them calmly and respectfully. Seek to understand what the person wants to achieve. In Stephen Covey's *The 7 Habits of Highly Effective People*, the fifth habit states that we must "seek first to understand, then to be understood". Give the person the benefit of the doubt. They may not realise you had a boundary in place.

Consider how you would respond to the following:

1. Someone who keeps telling sexist or racist jokes.
2. Someone who gossips about others.
3. Someone who constantly speculates about change to stir up drama.

Be tactful when dealing with these situations. Clearly and politely say:

1. "Everyone loves a good laugh. However, sexist and/or racist jokes are not funny."
2. "We really shouldn't be talking about that person. If you want to talk about them, then they should be here to be part of the conversation. Otherwise, it's gossip and I don't want you to get a reputation as the office gossip."
3. "That's interesting. Is it a fact or are you speculating? Who should we ask to get it verified?"

If someone discloses information about something

they shouldn't, you can address it with a blend of statement and question. You could politely say, "I'm not too sure if I'm meant to know that information. Is it public knowledge? It might be best not to continue telling me anything in case you're inadvertently breaching a policy, rule or confidence."

Pointing out when someone breaches a boundary does not mean you are whingeing or complaining. You are simply being clear about your boundaries. It means people will be less likely to breach them in the future.

If your boss makes an unreasonable request, the same steps apply. Seek to understand, then to be understood. Clarify their request and determine your next steps. For example, with a respectful tone, you could ask: "So that I understand more clearly what you're asking for, can you please give me some background and why you need this done now?"

Seek clarification, then either help your boss or respectfully explain your concrete boundary. It might be in your best interests to find someone else who can help them. You can still be helpful without bruising your boundaries!

Sometimes, you may be prepared to help someone with a task that dents your boundary. When this happens, let the person know you'll help them this time, but they will need to find an alternative strategy next time. If you continue to help them, you will resent the person for asking, as well as yourself for letting your boundary be breached.

Not everyone you work with is going to know your boundaries. It's up to you to determine how you will respond when this happens. For example, if someone emails you on the weekend, how would you react? Would you:

- Reply straight away?
- Respond on Monday (or your first day back at work), explaining you were on your weekend?
- Ignore it because you have your "out of office" switched on every weekend?

Don't be naive – be prepared for boundary violations. They will happen. Make sure your emotions are in check before you act. For example, if you receive a work email on a Saturday afternoon, what happens to your emotions when you see that email? Where do your thoughts go? Do your emotions drive an instant response or do you take a deep breath, think it through, and follow your own protocol around your boundaries? Make sure your actions match your boundaries. You don't want any heightened emotions to drive you to do anything you may later regret.

When I was a project officer with a constant flow of

people, problems, tasks and opportunities coming my way, a strategy that worked for me was to:

1. Take three 3/6 breaths. That is, breathe in for the count of three, then breathe out for the count of six. Do this three times. No one could tell I was doing this to calm myself.

2. Ask questions to make sure I clearly understood the situation.

3. Ask myself what category the request fitted into. Was it:
   - Not me?
   - Not now?
   - Never?

4. Take action by helping, delegating or explaining my boundary.

Like most things in life, it's all about balance! And just as building a fence takes time, so does building boundaries. It also takes practice.

TIPS FOR BOUNDARIES

1. Keep in mind that as the leader, you are a role model. Even if you don't expect your people to stay as late as you, many will feel an obligation to because they see you working late. Be explicit

about the expectations you have of your people and their working hours. There are rules about this for a reason. If you abuse your own working hours, you run the risk of abusing the boundaries of others' working hours, and you may get yourself into trouble.

2. When you allocate or delegate work, respect your employees' boundaries. Know that, in most cases, you will be adding more work on top of an already full capacity. Allocate the work and help the employee to reprioritise.

3. Be the voice of reason when ideas and opportunities are imposed upon you and your team. Explore the rationale behind the new work. Ask how the new work fits with core business, and be clear that to make way for the new work, something else will need to be dropped or delayed.

4. If you say no to an idea before you've weighed up its costs and benefits, then it's time to loosen the grip a little. The productive leader knows to listen, consider and challenge assumptions if necessary, *then* approve, delay or deny.

RELATIONSHIPS

Relationships need communication, period. Businesses are increasingly recognising the need to be better communicators and collaborators, as it helps them reach more diverse markets faster.

Positive, open and honest relationships are critical for success. Without professional, respectful relationships, there's no productivity. In fact, there's no organisation. A critical element of positive relationships – and getting work done – is effective communication. Underpinning all this is trust, and when you have the trust of your people, you can achieve great results.

A 2013 survey conducted by Hart Research Associates showed that 93% of employers considered good communication skills more important than a college graduate's major. Furthermore, the McKinsey Global Institute found that productivity improved by 20%-25% in an organisation with employees who felt connected. That kind of increase in productivity means a potential revenue of $1.3 trillion per year. That's 12 zeros! So, communication and relationships, connectedness and engagement, trust and openness mean increased productivity for increased revenue.

As our workforce changes with each generation, technology and globalisation, the nature of work and when and how it's done also changes. The workforce you joined will not look, feel or sound the same, and the interaction won't be the same, as the workforce you retire from. Relationships are key to ensuring an organisation's employees – even when they are dispersed globally – feel and act like one cohesive, high-functioning team.

Once when I was talking with a group of middle managers, I asked them what it would be like if they didn't have to talk to anyone at work. What if no one asked them what they were doing or how they were progressing? As you'd expect, almost all of them thought it would be delightful, a paradise! "No nagging, no interruptions, it would be a dream." I then asked them to consider how they would think and feel if they were in the same situation for six months. The mood shifted instantly. "I'd probably start to feel lonely and ignored," was the reply that summed up the room.

Relationships lie at the intersection of personal productivity and people productivity. One impacts the other every day.

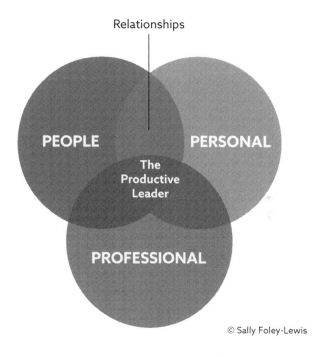

© Sally Foley-Lewis

One way of understanding the importance of relationships and how they link your personal and people productivity is to imagine you are a toy tester. Let's take LEGO as an example. You're the only LEGO toy tester in the world. You're it, no one else. At first, it's fantastic because you get all the LEGO to yourself. No one gets in your way, no one takes any pieces from you, no one pulls pieces off your creation to add to their own. It's a little slice of LEGO paradise.

But after a while, it's no longer as fun. You don't get to share. You don't get to swap or negotiate. You don't get to check out what others are doing to get ideas, you don't get to compete, you don't get to interact, you don't get to learn, you don't get feedback, and you don't get to share joy with others. You start to feel lonely and disengaged. Your productivity may not suffer greatly without relationships, but without others, you will never reach your productivity potential. Likewise, others need your input, insights and knowledge for their productivity as much as you need theirs.

A great mentor of mine talks about function over friendship. While the meaning is not literal, the lesson is worthy: if you can't have friendships – friendly relationships – at work, then the relationships must be mutually respectful of the functions each person performs. Respect for function is fundamental for building productive relationships. The productive leader builds on the respect they have for the roles others play and the outcomes each is trying to achieve.

This starts with the absolute basics: manners and appreciation. According to Globoforce, a provider of social recognition solutions, 78% of employees say they'd work harder if they were better appreciated and recognised (survey conducted in 2012). Please, thank you and hello are greatly appreciated, but they have disappeared from some workplaces.

The productive leader thinks about how they communicate their expectations to others. Research and consulting company Gallup's 2017 State of the American Workforce reports that six out of 10 employees know exactly what's expected of them, which means there are four out of 10 who are lost or unsure. Can your organisation, team or business afford 40% of the workforce to be unclear about what they're meant to be doing?

Clear expectations are about being explicit. You cannot assume others know or understand what you expect of them. Be as open and unambiguous as possible when stating the standards and outcomes expected. Furthermore, don't assume employees know they can come to you with questions. They may leave your office with the task you've set them, thinking you've given them all the relevant information. But when they get started on the task, they find they have many questions. The employee is unsure whether they should speak up and ask. They don't want to look stupid. They may take the risk of trying to work it out themselves and make serious errors. You need to be explicit and state to the employee, "You can come back to me with questions and I will come to you if more information becomes available."

Another productivity killer that hinges on relationships is the inability to follow up. So many managers and leaders admit that they don't follow up as much as they should. They want better engagement, better results and a more productive workforce, but they skip this key step that helps boost results. Nothing says you don't matter like a boss who never follows up! Why do the work if no one cares or checks?

Effective communication is the foundation of relationships. Listening is a major part of communication, yet it is often overlooked. The ability to listen is so important when it comes to learning, engaging and contributing to productivity. People want to know they've been heard. As a productive leader, the more you listen, the more you learn about the people in your team, the way they think, the work they're doing and the ideas they can contribute.

In today's organisation, the networks you have are key to surviving a crisis. The stronger your relationships across your organisation, the better you can work through a challenge together.

When you have quality relationships:

- You can give and receive support from peers across departments and across an industry.
- You can come together faster as a team to strategise and problem solve.
- You don't lose time, money or reputation in the market trying to gain rapport with other departments and employees before you can start fixing problems.

Showing an interest in what others do helps build a culture of reciprocity. If you show an interest in and help others, they are more likely to be interested in and help you. If you want to learn more about reciprocity in relationships, I highly recommend Robert Cialdini's classic, *Influence: The Psychology of Persuasion*.

The productive leader works to build and maintain quality relationships by:

- Listening and seeking to understand instead of assuming.
- Asking thoughtful, clarifying questions that inspire thinking.
- Encouraging problem solving and decision making with the right balance of support.
- Creating rapport by being interested in others rather than expecting others to be automatically interested in them.
- Meeting people without judgement.
- Building trust by being authentic.

One of the most enduring messages I've heard was during a leadership program in 2003: "You cannot hate the person whose story you know." This quote reminds me that when I take the time to learn about someone, I am the one who benefits. I get to learn what makes them tick and why they do what they do. In turn, this helps me engage with them at a far more productive level.

TIPS FOR BETTER RELATIONSHIPS

1. Listen! Quieten your mind-talk and listen! Don't make up your mind and second guess before you've heard the whole story, pitch or idea. If you want people to listen to you, you must listen when others speak. Truly listening ensures you have all the information you need to complete the work or achieve a goal.

2. In his excellent book *Stepping Up: How Taking Responsibility Changes Everything*, Dr John Izzo suggests that the more time leaders spend explaining the why behind a project, the greater level of understanding, acceptance and willingness to act the employees will have. Too often, managers dictate a task without nearly enough explanation as to why:

    - *"Because it has to be done."*
    - *"Because the CEO wants it."*
    - *"Because I said so."*

    These explanations are unacceptable. The productive leader seeks to understand the "why" so they can inform their people. The why is the glue that binds and strengthens the team to the task.

3. The productive leader knows that they do not have all the answers. Productive leaders know

their people probably know more about the work being done than they do, so they will ask their people what changes, opportunities and ideas will work best.

Managers who are promoted into a leadership role often assume they will have all the answers. Their self-talk is usually along the lines of, "They promoted me, therefore I should know."

In no policy manual, procedures folder or workplace intranet has it ever been written:

"YOU'VE BEEN PROMOTED SO THEREFORE YOU MUST KNOW!"

Remember to:

- Ask questions.
- Build an internal network with other leaders.
- Encourage your people to think by coaching them rather than giving direct answers when they come to you looking for answers.

4. Trust. It takes years to build, seconds to break, and forever to repair. Always be mindful of building trust amongst your team. Start with trusting yourself! Trust and respect grow when your actions and words are aligned.

DOING LESS MEANINGLESS WORK, SO THAT YOU CAN FOCUS ON THINGS OF GREATER PERSONAL IMPORTANCE, IS NOT LAZINESS. THIS IS HARD FOR MOST PEOPLE TO ACCEPT, BECAUSE OUR CULTURE TENDS TO REWARD PERSONAL SACRIFICE INSTEAD OF PERSONAL PRODUCTIVITY.

– TIMOTHY FERRISS

WARNING!

Here is the fine print, the terms and conditions, the exclusions from warranty per se …

As you dive into the pages of this book to boost your productive leadership, be warned: successful outcomes take effort!

There, it has been said. You will need to put effort in to get the results out. There is no sugar-coating this and if you work with me as a client or if you've been in any of my audiences, you'll know that sugar-coating is not my style.

And as you apply the tips and strategies suggested in the following pages, you should also be prepared for the following:

- Generally, the first time you try something new, it feels clunky, awkward and may not go as you imagined. That's quite normal. I often suggest that if it doesn't feel a little odd, you might not be trying hard enough. One of the best ways to think of this is that the first time is always the worst, so get it out of the way quickly. Practice with a trusted colleague.

- Even with the most admirable and well-intended actions, approaches, words and sentiments, you cannot guarantee others will understand, appreciate or support you. This may be because you are doing something so out of character, something so different to how they see you, it surprises or shocks them. It may be because you are evolving and developing and they feel threatened. It may be because they just don't get it or care. It may be their shock is actually delightful surprise. If you know that the changes you make to improve your productivity and productive leadership are the right ones, don't let any potential negative reactions sway you from your course.

Does this mean you should give up? No! No! No! Why? Because you're worth the effort. Any action that is taken to improve should be trialled, tested, tweaked where necessary and tried again. If a strategy doesn't work the first time, stop and reflect on why. Seek input from those who are impacted. Remember, no one jumps into a swimming pool and instantly swims a world record-breaking 100m freestyle!

Avoid focusing on the time it takes to improve your productive leadership. Instead, see it as an investment. Just like saving money, there is a compounding effect. The time, value and energy you'll get back will definitely pay you back two-fold, or more!

TIP:

Let people know your intentions. When people know what you're aiming for, they will have more information on hand to support you, guide you, or at the very least stay out of your way. Stating your intentions minimises the surprise and shock of a new behaviour that others may not initially understand.

If you're not sure about where to start, you can always email me at sally@sallyfoleylewis.com.

SALLY FOLEY-LEWIS

PART 1

PERSONAL PRODUCTIVITY

Personal productivity is all about you. Self-leadership is at its very core.

It helps to start by answering the following questions:

1. What's in the way of getting what I want done?
2. Is what I'm doing what I really want to do, or do I just want to want it?
3. Why do I procrastinate? What snaps me out of procrastination?
4. What makes me lose focus, stop paying attention or fail to be present?
5. What is the value I place on my time and effort?

Personal productivity is about leading yourself through the distractions and multiple demands to maintain calm and focus to achieve – if not exceed – results. When you look at your personal productivity, do you ensure you are focused and able to prioritise yourself using effective scheduling? Do you schedule time for thinking and self-care?

It's also about balance over the long term and being able to meet the peaks and troughs of shifting demands. Self-awareness is critical for minimising unproductive habits and time wasters. The productive leader identifies their procrastination triggers and acts to eliminate them. When fully present, the productive leader can engage, influence and achieve more in terms of efficiency, time and energy.

This is all about you! Scheduling you! It involves understanding your habits, your focus and attention.

The next section of this book focuses on five ways to understand and boost your personal productivity. Without these key elements, your leadership journey and your ability to get the work done and successfully lead a team are much more difficult to achieve:

1. Busy versus achievement
2. Habits and individual time wasters
3. Focus and attention
4. Procrastination
5. Scheduling you

CHAPTER 3

BUSY VERSUS ACHIEVEMENT

The sense of feeling rushed, the sense of being busy, is partly a perception problem. That perception is incredibly influenced by the fact that we work less hours than our great grandparents did. In Australia, we're down to a 38-hour ordinary working week; even though many employees work more than that and their leaders even more so.

Unpaid work, such as household chores, is still handled predominately by women. However, men are doing more than they ever did. Furthermore, innovation has made unpaid work more efficient and convenient: we can access dishwashers, automatic washing machines and dryers, microwaves and food-delivery services like never before.

Spending is focused on making life easier, yet we've never felt more rushed and busy.

What's happened is that when the clock synchronised in the 18th century to sort and control labour, it marked the beginning of linking time with money. We work more to buy more to make life easier.

When we think about leisure time, the question arises: how does leisure time chew into the ability to make money and be prosperous? If leisure time does not add to our prosperity or make money, it needs to be as productive as possible. And so begins the start of synchronising activities during leisure time. It's no secret that many of us sit in front of a television, iPad in one hand, eating dinner with the other, while keeping an eye on another mobile device. These activities start to rob one's leisure time.

History teaches us that being busy can make you rich. The problem with this is that you feel you must constantly be busy. Being busy means that you can make money.

But the big question is, with all this busy-ness, what are you achieving? What is success? Is it all about a bank balance? For some, the answer will be yes. For others, it will be no. Get this clear first so you can productively shift from busy to achievement.

It's important to clarify what "busy" and "achievement" mean. The clock was the key to synchronised labour as it linked time with money for the first time. So, it's essential that we look at what work is being done when it comes to evaluating the return on our effort and time. It is an age-old issue: the more the work is valued, the higher the reach in prosperity, and the more value is placed on time. Furthermore, the more importance we place on not wasting time. The knock-on effect is that people are busy or being seen to be busy, and managers want to see busy people.

Some people are cursed with too much leisure time. They struggle to find ways to fill their time that give them a sense of achievement. Others find it too costly to enjoy their time. Many spend their spare moments staring at a screen rather than engaging in fulfilling activities, such as volunteering and being present with friends and family. Activities that connect humans make us happier.

With busy work time and busy leisure time, we don't stop nearly enough to check whether we are achieving – or what the achievement is.

High Achievement

Works hard and then works even harder!

- Sporadic planning, prioritising and reviewing.
- Knows there is a better way but not sure what or how.
- Gets results but pays heavily for them.

Works hard, smart and calm!

- Plans, prioritises and has goals: can see the big picture.
- Seeks advice and support.
- Delegates.
- Knows own boundaries and guards them well.
- Has focus and attention.
- Learns from mistakes: reflects, reviews and continuously develops.

Busy — **Busy v Achievement** — **Productive**

As the saying goes: "Flogging a dead horse!"

- Invisible.
- Exhausted.
- No direction, goals, plan or priorities.
- Repeats mistakes.
- Lacks big picture.

When deciding inaction

- When all consideration leads to the right, the more productive outcome being to *not* act.
- Stopping a project leads to greater returns.
- It will most likely look like low achievement for the halted project with a productivity boost showing up in another project.

© Sally Foley-Lewis

Low Achievement

QUADRANT 1: HIGH ACHIEVING AND BUSY

When you have a high level of achievement and lots of activity – that is, you're busy – (quadrant 1), it's wise to ask if you're working hard enough for the returns you're getting. This might be difficult to assess because although you're achieving, you often don't pay attention to what it costs you to get the achievement. When operating from this quadrant, you may engage in sporadic planning, prioritising and reviewing. There may be a lack of goal clarity. You may know there's a better way but not sure what that is, how to start or how to stop what you're doing to shift to the more productive way. You may have constraints that hinder you from operating in a more productive way (if so, please re-read Chapter 2).

When you operate from quadrant 1, it's like you're on a treadmill. You're too scared to stop the treadmill because if you do, the results won't come, the achievements won't come. The answer is counter-intuitive. If you stop the treadmill and create a plan or review an existing plan and prioritise, you'll shift over into being high achieving *and* productive. It will help you stop the busy, unnecessary work so you can get on with the productive work.

QUADRANT 3: LOW ACHIEVING AND BUSY

If you have a low level of achievement and are super

busy (quadrant 3), you are, as the saying goes, flogging a dead horse. Everything you do feels invisible. You're exhausted. You don't have direction. You don't plan. You don't prioritise. Maybe you don't know how to do all these things, which leads you to repeating mistakes. You feel that you don't have time to lift your head to see what's going on around you or to take advantage of opportunities that might help you be more productive. You aren't focused on the big picture.

Again, it's counter-intuitive, but when you do stop to review and plan, you leave the unproductive busy work behind. You make better choices that lead to more productive and more fulfilling, achievement-laden work. John Wooden, who is an American legend as a basketball player and coach, is famously quoted as saying, "Don't mistake activity with achievement." You can't get clearer than that.

If you or your team operates from quadrant 1 or 3, the most effective tasks you can do as a productive leader are, first, stop! Review what you are doing. Help the team review their work. Review or create a plan. Work the plan! Do what a quadrant 2 operator would do!

QUADRANT 2: HIGH ACHIEVING AND WORKS SMART

When you work hard, smart and calm – that is, when you operate from quadrant 2 – you plan and prioritise. You seek advice and support. You learn how to delegate. You put your boundaries in place and you focus more and for longer. The activities you and the team do are of value and give you a return. You learn from your mistakes. You and your team reflect and review so you constantly learn and develop. You keep your eye on the big picture.

How do you work out what to do? You choose:

BUSY PEOPLE	PRODUCTIVE LEADERS
Write a plan and stick to it no matter what.	Write a plan but stay flexible so they are agile when – not if – a crisis or better opportunity arises.
Put their head down and keep working.	Look up and see what's going on around them.
Struggle to link their day-to-day activities with the bigger organisational picture. They tend to operate with a silo mentality as they've not given themselves permission or time to look up, network, learn and make the connections.	Know that building networks across the organisation is beneficial for knowing who to turn to when help is needed, and who to turn to because someone else has the skills needed for a certain task. *Continued next page*

From previous page Stick to procedures that have been in place for a long time.	Follow procedures while also being open to and exploring potential improvements to save time, effort and resources.
Have a to-do list with 20+ items to demonstrate they are busy.	Keep their to-do list realistic so as not to overwhelm and interrupt meaningful work from being achieved.
Do lots of tasks quickly, not stopping to check quality, just checking them off as they go.	Do the important tasks right and first-ish* time. *"First-ish" means sometimes there are tweaks and there might be a need to come back and redraft. However, there's less fixing if there's a focus on doing it right the first time and slowing down enough to give the task its due attention.
Say yes to everything because that will keep them busy in the eyes of those they wish to impress.	Carefully consider the implications of saying yes before taking on the new task. *Continued next page*

From previous page Are affected by FOMO – Fear of Missing Out. They have all the notifications switched on for emails, text messages, phone calls and social media posts.	Allocate or schedule time for emails, calls and productive work.
Assume others are also busy so they don't delegate, ask for help or check if they are doing something the correct or most productive way.	Realise everyone is different so they will ask questions, learn about other people's workload and what they would like to do more or less of to be more productive.
Believe it's important to be seen as busy.	Know the results speak for themselves.

Which do you choose?

QUADRANT 4: LOW ACHIEVING AND PRODUCTIVE

Does low achievement with high productivity make sense? Prima facie, not so much! Whether the focus of achievement is on you, your team or the organisation as whole, low levels of achievement won't be tolerated for long. That's obvious. The situation where low achievement and high productivity might seem feasible is when a decision to not pursue a project or task has resulted in a boost to productivity. Although the project has been rejected, the result is that the team's effort and attention are positively or profitably diverted elsewhere, thus boosting productivity in another area or on another project or task.

TAKING BACK TIME!

A state government department was divided into three teams: policy, project and program. The program team had one key program to deliver, so its deliverables were singular and obvious. The policy team similarly had clear deliverables, albeit somewhat impacted by needing to be responsive to the minister's needs (and political moods). The project team, however, was constantly pulled in multiple directions to be involved in, take charge of and initiate projects for a range of stakeholders covering a range of geographies across the state. If you worked in the project team, you hardly had time to warm your chair, you were that busy!

While the argument for the diversity of projects could be made, the reality was that the team was being stretched too thin, delivering okay to good quality, and with attentions scattered.

Through a review and planning process, the project team worked hard to let go of projects that were not delivering enough impact for its mandate. Naturally, some team members struggled to let go of initiatives they felt invested in. However, the whole process was managed well and within a few weeks, the project team was less busy because they were achieving.

The result was increased stakeholder engagement,

increased "feel-good" stories (press release potential) for the minister, more funding for the right projects and improved staff morale.

One team member, who admitted to struggling with letting go of one particular project, noted that within a few weeks, he realised the project had not been returning enough of an impact and they were now glad it been dropped. This same team member also noticed that he had time to read and engage deeper in other projects. He estimated an extra four hours per week were taken back to be reinvested in more valuable activities.

PLANNING HELPS ACHIEVEMENT BEAT OUT BUSY!

"Planning is boring."
"I thought I was clear on what I had to do."
"Too much time is wasted talking and not doing."

The reality is that a lack of planning leads to mistakes, wasted resources and backtracking. This means the whole exercise takes even longer than if some planning had been done prior to implementation. No planning leads to an easy descent into busy!

Planning is only boring if you are not aligned with the desired outcome. Ask yourself what would bring you the most satisfaction and best return on your effort and input. Planning is ineffective if you do not make the goal clear, specific and with a direction. Write specific goals that are measurable, check that they have the right balance of challenge and achievability, and set a specific time limit.

Remember, as discussed in Chapter 2, writing SMART goals is the most effective format:

- Specific
- Measurable
- Attainable
- Realistic
- Time bound

MANAGING YOUR TIME
WITHOUT SETTING PRIORITIES
IS LIKE SHOOTING RANDOMLY
AND CALLING WHATEVER YOU
HIT THE TARGET.

– PETER TURLA

CHAPTER 4

HABITS AND INDIVIDUAL TIME WASTERS

Habits can help or hinder. What is the first thing you do in the morning? Many people grab their mobile device to check emails and social media before they even roll out of bed.

Is this a helpful habit? Only you know the truth to that. Only you know if this gets you excited to start your day or if it places a heavy burden on you before you've even dragged yourself out of bed. Only you know if giving more attention to emails and social media when you get home each evening and throughout your weekend is more fulfilling than spending quality time with your loved ones.

Was that enough of a guilt trip for you?

The way to get rid of an unproductive habit is to replace it with a more helpful, healthy or productive habit. In his book *The Power of Habit*, Charles Duhigg explains how MIT researchers in the early 1990s discovered the habit loop. This loop consists of a cue, a routine and a reward. To change a habit, you need to identify the cues and the rewards. Once you can pinpoint these, you can change the routine.

Time wasters are a type of habit. They are activities that get in the way of your productivity, minimising achievement and success. They are a means of procrastinating, and they can be subconsciously driven. The key is to observe and identify, then make changes.

Self-awareness is your most fundamental requirement for success! Reflecting on your behaviour and auditing your behaviour, routines and habits helps you identify and reduce individual time wasters.

There are two types of time wasters. External time wasters are those activities that impact you but you cannot always control them. You can certainly influence them, though. External time wasters will be covered in Part 2 of this book. Individual time wasters, which are covered here, impact your personal productivity because they are the activities you have total control over. These time wasters are akin to self-sabotage. You can start, modify or stop them at any time: with decision, discipline and determination. Both types of time wasters do not serve you well.

Research from CareerBuilder, 2014, shows that at least one quarter of workers surveyed spend at least an hour a day on personal emails, texts and calls. Other time wasters included in the research were:

- Gossiping
- Social media
- Surfing the internet
- Snack breaks or smoke breaks

This is just the tip of the time-wasting iceberg. There are numerous ways in which people can waste their time, and they vary wildly. For your entertainment, here are a few you might enjoy knowing about (of course, you don't do any of these):

- Caring for pets that get smuggled into the office.
- Personal grooming in the office bathrooms – eg. shaving.
- Playing games, such as hide and seek and wrestling with co-workers.
- Photocopying a text book.
- Printing off a book from the internet.
- Surfing dating sites on the internet.
- Online gambling.

These are all real examples of people who have been *caught* wasting time.

Time wasters and habits are related because a time waster can easily become a habit if repeated enough. Time wasters happen for myriad reasons: boredom, lack of focus, waiting for someone or something, avoiding something, to name a few. Time wasters are also the activities we engage in while procrastinating.

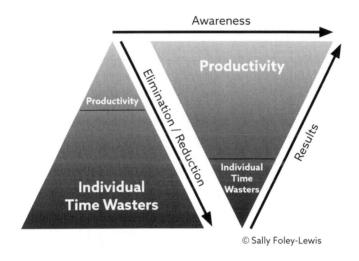

© Sally Foley-Lewis

Time wasters are like an equal opportunity employer, as described by Denis Waitley in *The Joy of Working*:

> *Time is an equal opportunity employer. Each human being has exactly the same number of hours and minutes every day. Rich people can't buy more hours. Scientists can't invent new minutes. And you can't save time to spend it on another day. Even so, time is amazingly fair and forgiving. No matter how much time you've wasted in the past, you still have an entire tomorrow.*

If you believe you don't waste time, then ask someone you trust to give their opinion of how you spend your time. Be warned, do not shoot the messenger if you hear something you do not like! Keep in mind that asking a trusted colleague this question is designed to help you increase your self-awareness so you can eliminate your time wasters.

Take five minutes to audit yourself. What are your time wasters? No one else needs to see the list; it's for your eyes only. Once you identify the activities that do not serve you, you can act to eliminate them.

If your list overwhelms you, that may be a good thing. Let it be the motivation to help you be more productive. If you can see your time wasters are driven by boredom, then it's time you looked at the work you are engaged to do and find ways to build in more challenging and exciting work. That may even mean finding a new job.

As time wasters are closely related to habits, it's important to identify what triggers you to engage in your time waster. As an example, a client told me that when they know they have a stack of reading to do, a trigger goes off and prompts them to make a cup of tea or coffee. Instead of starting the reading straight away, their habit is to put it off for a few minutes and make a cuppa. They admitted that often while making the beverage, they think of another task they could do, again delaying the reading. Do they need the beverage? Hardly ever! Is it an individual time waster? In this context, absolutely!

Having an accountability partner for eliminating time wasters is incredibly helpful. Partner with someone you trust who would appreciate what you aim to achieve. Share with them your time wasters list, what you plan to eliminate and what you will do instead. Start by eliminating one time waster so you can make the change stick. Tell your accountability partner how you want to be held accountable – do not assume they know. This is your productivity, so step up and take charge. Remember, constant small steps lead to big transformations!

There are numerous applications and programs you can download that can block, delete or minimise your access to your mobile device or computer if using it (to check social media and email, for example) is mostly a time waster for you.

Changing habits to improve productivity takes real effort. There's no magic wand. Make friends with discipline and determination. Once you know what triggers a habitual behaviour and the results you seek, you are able to experiment with different, more productive behaviours to get more positive rewards.

WILLPOWER AND PRACTICE

Willpower is not everlasting. It can be depleted. Don't rely on willpower to be your only productivity tool.

As Vince Lombardi, a famous football coach, once said, "Practice does not make perfect. Only perfect practice makes perfect." Focus on **more deliberate** practice. Break the skill down so you can get each part right. Lombardi is also quoted as saying, "Perfection is unattainable, but if we chase perfection we can catch excellence." Use these sentiments as motivators: know when you've reached excellence.

Focus on practicing the toughest components of the skill, then build the components up so you reach excellence in the whole skill.

TIPS:

1. Use short breaks between longer working sessions to improve focus and productivity.

2. To be more productive, start. Starting is generally the biggest roadblock. Once you know your goal and the outcome you're working towards, bring your focus back to the first step and build momentum. Don't let the image of the end result, that big goal, overwhelm you into inactivity!

TAKING BACK TIME!

Following a productivity audit, Georgia realised that she spent more time on tasks than she had assumed. She also realised she spent more time proofreading other people's work than she thought she should.

The audit kickstarted a review of how proofreading would be handled by the team before it got to Georgia's desk. The change in process resulted in Georgia gaining back an average of 45 minutes per day. Just from the proofreading alone, Georgia took back three hours and 45 minutes in her week!

"I never have enough time!"

As Dan Norris says in his short yet excellent book, *Create or Hate*: "If you are living in a free country, all time is 'free' and you make the decision how to allocate that time."

Think about that, then decide in favour of yourself and what you want to achieve.

CHAPTER 5

FOCUS AND ATTENTION

Quality = focus + attention + time

When you focus on what you're doing, when you consciously pay attention to the task in front of you, the quality of the output will improve.

In Daniel Goleman's book, *Focus*, he talks about voluntary attention, or top-down thinking. This is where you are in control, purposefully trying things. With voluntary attention, you deliberately think and use your focus and attention. You actively work to ignore distractions so you can concentrate on a task.

Think of voluntary attention as a muscle. It needs training and it needs care. When we use top-down thinking, as Goleman says, it might be slow but you are in control. Top-down thinking is full of effort, the seat of self-control. It is the part of the brain that works towards overcoming our automatic routines, habits and impulses. This is the part of the mind that creates and learns new ways of doing things. It plans and, to a certain extent, takes charge of our automatic behaviours.

Goleman also introduces us to the bottom-up brain. This is involuntary thinking based on impulse: it's emotionally driven. It's the part of the brain that makes sure we stick to our habits and routines. It operates on intuition and the associations we have embedded throughout our life.

The best way to understand the involuntary mind is to think of what happens to us when the doorbell rings or an email pops up in our inbox. Our attention is instantly drawn to it no matter what we are doing.

Putting these two minds in the context of focus and attention, the average employee is interrupted by a phone call every three minutes. We live in a world of distractions. Add to this the relentless push for results, it is no wonder attention spans are getting shorter and focus is much harder to achieve.

Distractions will always be present. While you can eliminate some permanently and others temporarily, your ability to focus and pay attention to a task despite distractions is key to successful personal productivity.

According to a 2017 Harvard Business Review article, employees and leaders do not have time-management issues – rather, they have attention-management issues. The skills to maintain focus and attention have been eroded by constant distractions and the push to be busy at the sacrifice of productivity and achievement.

If your attention to tasks varies as much as the quality and results you get, you may be doing the wrong work or work you don't have the skillset for yet. You may be bored or overwhelmed, which leads to procrastination. However, there are times when you can achieve great results with seemingly little focus. It may be because of luck, or it may be an easy task or a highly systematised or regulated task that requires you to follow stringent steps.

The aim is for what famous Hungarian psychologist Mihaly Csikszentmihalyi calls "flow". Flow is when you are in your groove. You're lost in the moment, totally absorbed in the task. When you are in flow, nothing else matters.

DISTRACTIONS

1. Look around you and notice the distractions: sounds, lights, smells, clutter. Determine which of these you can remove, even if temporarily. Notice the distractions you cannot control. Acknowledge that you have little influence over these to avoid giving them more energy than necessary.

2. Turn off the bells, whistles, dings and push notifications on your technology. Pay attention to all

the little add-ons with applications (apps), software and technology, which are meant to grab your attention and redirect you from the quality work you should be doing.

3. Take three deep breaths: breathe in to a calmly paced count of three and breathe out to a calmly paced count of six. This is about calming emotions and helping you prepare. Plus, it oxygenates your brain.

4. Set your intention. That is, be clear and specific about the task you need to do. What is the result you want? Complete this sentence: By the end of this _____ minute block, I will have successfully completed _____.

5. Set a timer for how long you will work on that task. Go!

Alternatively, explore where you could go to be away from the distractions. A lot of workplaces have meeting rooms, vacant offices or small outdoor courtyards that can provide a respite from some of the more distracting noises.

TIMERS

The highly popular Pomodoro Technique, developed in the late 1980s, suggests working in 25-minute intervals with short breaks in between and a longer break after a series of four 25-minute blocks. The name comes from a kitchen timer that was in the shape of a pomodoro tomato. This is a great strategy if your day-to-day is often broken up into small pockets of time – for example, if you have lots of meetings interspersed with 20- to 30-minute time gaps.

If your daily calendar has larger gaps, then you can build your "attention management muscle" by increasing the times you spend on single-intention tasks. Ultradian rhythm is a recurrent period or cycle that is repeated throughout a day. The term is used in sleep research and refers to the 90- to 120-minute sleep cycles during human sleep. Using this cycle as a personal productivity technique can be advantageous. Tony Schwartz, bestselling author and CEO of The Energy Project, advocates working for 90 minutes, then having a 20-minute break.

BREAKS

It may seem counter-intuitive, but the truth is that to have more focus and be more attentive to your work, you need to have breaks. The quality of your break is important, too. Your break should involve something completely different from your work. If you've been working at your desk, get up and stretch or go for a short walk. If you've been doing physically taxing work, stretch, sit, and read or listen to music that will boost concentration. Try the productivity app focus@ will (www.focusatwill.com) to find the right music for you.

Avoid matching the activity and energy level of your break with your work. Take this example: If you finish a work activity after 90 minutes, then go to a busy shopping mall or walk around a busy city street during your break, you're not giving yourself time to relax. You're adding more stimuli to your involuntary attention, which drains your already taxed voluntary attention that you've been using for your work. Because you're in this busy environment during your break, you need to decide what you do and don't need to pay attention to: street and pedestrian safety, what to buy, avoiding shopping trolleys, loud music in the stores, etc.

Your break needs to re-energise you – not tax you.

COMMUNICATE TO OTHERS

Manage others' expectations by letting the relevant people know you are working on something that needs a deeper level of concentration. Help them to help you. Don't assume that people can see you're working on something that requires intense attention. Quite often, people don't know. They may also be deeply focused on their own work, which means if they need something from you they will fail to see any non-verbal signs from you that you're busy. Hence the interruption of, "Have you got a second?" or "Can I pick your brain for a moment?"

GENERAL HEALTH AND WELLBEING

Sleep, drink water and exercise. Regular check-ups are important to ensure you are on top of your health. Exercise according to what is right for you. Make sure you get expert advice prior to starting any new exercise routine.

Look after you. If you're constantly having late nights, your attention will diminish over the course of the week. Make sure you get rest. And drink water to keep your body hydrated.

ARE THEY INTERRUPTIONS? OR ARE THEY REQUIREMENTS OF YOUR JOB?

I was facilitating a productivity program with a group of administration professionals. As we got onto the topic of interruptions and time wasters, Yasmina said to me: "The biggest thing I hate about my job is answering the phone. I'm constantly interrupted by phone calls."

I responded to Yasmina with a question, as I thought answering the phone was a major component of their role. I started to second-guess my understanding of what this group's functions were.

"Is answering the phone on behalf of your senior leader, team or department part of your role?" Yasmina confirmed my assumption. "Yes, it's in my job description."

I challenged Yasmina to review her mindset. I suggested that she stop describing phone calls as interruptions and start thinking of them as key tasks. I also encouraged her to focus on how well she answered the phone: being quick to answer, answering with a smile in her voice, quickly and accurately forwarding calls, and providing exceptional customer service. By doing this, she would be able to finish every day feeling proud of her valuable phone-management skills.

THE LESSON:

Once you acknowledge that an "interruption" is a key component of your job, you will notice a shift in energy. The task is no longer a negative – indeed, it can be a huge positive.

You may not be able to predict when you'll need to do the task, such as answering the phone. But because you're expecting it, you'll be able to accept it rather than feel annoyed when it does ring. Being prepared means you can factor phone calls into your plan for the day.

TIP:

If there are other staff members you can share tasks with, it will give you a chance to have some uninterrupted time. You can time trade! You could offer to answer someone else's phone for one hour so they can complete an important piece of work, then they can do the same for you. This may not work in all workplaces but it has worked in quite a few where I've challenged the teams to trial it.

TAKING BACK TIME!

Once Denis told the team when he wanted to be left alone so he could work on a task, his focus and attention improved dramatically. He would organise someone to cover his phone calls for a set period of time so he could get the work done without interruptions. He admitted that asking his team to cover him meant he needed to honour them by doing the work!

Denis observed that by setting up the team and himself for focus time, he completed reports faster than before. "It's like my report-completing muscle has been getting a workout and it's really fit now," Denis said. He calculated that reports that once took a few hours spread over a week now took between 35 and 50 minutes, saving him hours each week.

THE SIMPLE ACT OF PAYING
ATTENTION CAN TAKE YOU A
LONG, LONG WAY.

– KEANU REEVES

CHAPTER 6

PROCRASTINATION

In the words of poet Edward Young, procrastination is the thief of time. Procrastination is delaying actions and replacing high-priority tasks with lower-priority or more enjoyable tasks until a later time. When you put off tasks, especially important tasks, you feel a sense of guilt, which leads to a decrease in motivation and personal productivity. And this can create stress, especially if deadlines are missed. You risk disapproval from team members and management. Jobs are on the line when this happens and continues to happen.

- Guilt
- Motivation
- Personal productivity
- Stress
- Disapproval for missing deadlines and not meeting commitments.

© Sally Foley-Lewis

According to an article in *Psychology Today* (2008), 20% of adults admit to procrastinating. This percentage may be even higher, but people may not have completed the surveys because they were procrastinating! In 1978, 5% of people surveyed called themselves chronic procrastinators, whereas today it's 20%. Forty per cent of people have also reported experiencing a financial loss purely to their own procrastination. That's why it's so important to pay attention to what triggers procrastination.

Everyone is prone to some form of procrastination at some time. Even if you don't procrastinate often, you will have work colleagues who do – or staff, or even your own senior leaders. The tips and tools in this book can help you to help your colleagues minimise procrastination.

To improve your productivity, identify the tasks you procrastinate on. What are the triggers? What excuses do you give yourself? Do you procrastinate because you're demotivated? Or are you demotivated because you procrastinate? Knowing the answers to these questions means you can do something about it.

Procrastination is not a flaw in your character. It's a learned behaviour that, at some point in your past, has paid off for you. Avoiding something you don't want to deal with immediately is rewarding for the short term. But in the long term, it creates guilt, low motivation, high stress and lower productivity. Understanding your triggers will help you overcome procrastination. Naturally, some tasks spark triggers while others don't. Let's have a look at those triggers.

THE 7 PROCRASTINATION TRIGGERS AND HOW TO OVERCOME THEM

There are seven common triggers of procrastination. Read through the following questions and self-assess the strength or weakness of each trigger. Keep in mind that you might have a trigger that manifests for certain tasks but not others. For example, filing is a common task that triggers feelings of boredom and pointlessness. And failing to seek advice about a project can lead to multiple procrastination triggers, such as being afraid of success or failure, not knowing how to proceed and feeling overwhelmed. Use the tips for each trigger to create an action plan that minimises your roadblocks to productivity.

1. FEELING OVERWHELMED

You know you are overwhelmed by a task when you engage in negative self-talk, such as:

- *"This seems like a lot of work and I'm not sure I can cope with it all."*
- *"What if this turns out far worse than it sounds?"*
- *"I don't want to even think about it!"*

Self-Assessment Questions:

Do you feel you don't have enough:

- Training to complete the task?
- Time to complete the task?
- Experience to complete the task?

Tips for Overcoming the Overwhelm:

- Determine/measure the actual work involved.
- Break the task into sub-tasks of time and re-sources.
- If the scope of the task becomes larger than an-ticipated, present the issue to your manager as soon as possible. They may be able to assist you with reprioritising or task sharing.

2. AFRAID OF SUCCESS

This is one trigger many people struggle to admit to. Success is usually considered a good thing! You may think, *"Why would anyone admit to fearing success?"* Success can lead to the scary "unknown".

Self-Assessment Questions:

If you successfully complete this task, do you fear you will:

- Be "rewarded" (punished) with another task that's more difficult?
- Be promoted?
- Alienate your peers?
- Be moved to another team or department?
- Make others look bad?

Tips for Making Friends with Success:

- Consider whether your fear is of the unknown rather than actual success. It may be that you're worried you will be promoted or shifted from your current team to an unknown situation.
- Having a great external and internal network is important. It means you can ask colleagues what it's like to work in different areas.
- Ask your manager what you may be rewarded with and share your feelings.
- A mentor, someone who has been there before, can help you work through this procrastination trigger by sharing their first-hand experience of handling success.

3. RESENT RESPONSIBILITY

This trigger may be a consequence of something else rather than a primary cause of procrastination. For example, you may feel the task is boring, disagreeable, pointless, unclear or overwhelming, so it makes sense that you would resent the responsibility of the task.

Self-Assessment Questions:

- Is the task appropriate to your job title and role description?
- Do you believe someone else should be responsible for completing the task?
- Do you feel you're not being rewarded appropriately given the level of responsibility?

Tips to Help Dull the Resentment:

- Ask yourself if you are being realistic about the responsibilities of your job.
- You may not be able to get out of doing the task this time, or at all, so consider what actions or hints you may have given to indicate you wanted the task. If you're not sure, ask. If you've established why you were assigned the task yet still think you're the wrong person for the job, consider discussing how you might delegate the task to the most appropriate person. This is not a suggestion to "palm off" the task to just anyone. Be realistic and respectful. The task needs to be done and it needs to be done by the right person.

4. AFRAID OF FAILURE

This trigger may come about because you feel the task is beyond your abilities, or that the results won't be up to what is expected.

Self-Assessment Questions:

- Do you feel there's a significant chance you'll fail to achieve what's expected?
- Do you feel there are factors beyond your control that will likely cause you to fail?
- Do you feel you'll be judged on the outcome of the task by your manager or peers?

Tips to Help You Kick Failure to the Kerb:

- Check details with all stakeholders. Make sure everyone is aware of any concerns or reservations. Think about when the best time would be to play devil's advocate or raise questions.
- Phrase concerns in a positive way, such as through seeking clarifications. Framing your concern or reservation in a question minimises the potential for others to become instantly defensive.
- Discuss the details face to face where possible and follow up by capturing and emailing all details to everyone involved. This covers everyone, not just yourself, for future hiccups.
- Keep key people up to date with your progress so you can avoid unexpected – and unwanted – surprises.

5. UNSURE HOW TO PROCEED

This is a powerful procrastination trigger most of us

have experienced. Consider whether you ever find yourself thinking:

"I'm not sure I'm allowed to make those decisions."
"I'm missing a lot of information about this."
"I don't know which is the best way to go."

Self-Assessment Questions:

- Do you feel unclear about the expected outcome?
- Are you unsure of exactly what's required to perform the task?
- Do you feel you could start if you had a clearly defined first step?

Tips to Help You Work Out the Way Forward:

- Speak to your manager to clarify what level of responsibility and decision-making authority you have for the task.
- Consider that there are often many ways to achieve a task. Sometimes, you simply need to start to work out the next steps.
- Ask the relevant stakeholders or your peers for their input.
- Share your options with your manager to get some guidance.
- Be prepared to find the solution through trial and error.

6. AFRAID OF CONFLICT/CONFRONTATION

Very few people enjoy confrontation. People perceive the intensity of confrontation differently and it is quite literally personal: what one person sees as a terrible, destructive confrontation may be perceived as a healthy, robust debate by someone else. Culture also plays a part in how people perceive conflict and confrontation.

Self-Assessment Questions:

- Will the task involve a confrontation (or conflict) with a:
  - Co-worker?
  - Workmate?
  - Customer?
  - Supplier?
  - Manager/senior leader?

Tips to Help You Confront Confrontation or Conflict:

- Ensure you clearly state the task objective and intention of your actions so that if you are confronted, you can circle the conversation back to the objective or intention.
- Communicate without blame or judgement.
- Talk about the issue or behaviour rather than the person. Name behaviours that impact your task

achievement without attacking, blaming or judging the people/person.

- If a similar conflict has arisen between other people, ask them how they handled the conflict.
- Research conflict resolution strategies. If the conflict is extreme, speak to your HR representative to assist you with building conflict resolution skills. A resource such as the Conflict Dynamics Profile helps individuals and teams understand how conflict affects them. If it is an ongoing issue that negatively impacts morale and productivity, please do consider an assessment.

7. POINTLESS/BORING TASK

This may be the most common trigger of procrastination across the world!

Self-Assessment Questions:

- Do you feel the output or results of the task will be ignored or not acted on?
- Do you feel the task fails to utilise your potential?
- Do you feel the task is beneath your skill level?
- Are you unclear about the reason/s why the task needs to be completed?
- Have you done this task repeatedly and lost all interest in it?

Tips to Beat the Boredom:

- If it's a one-off task, it's probably easier to simply get on with it. It may be difficult to justify it away.
- If the task is beneath you, consider who is the right person based on skills, time and responsibility. Be realistic.
- Consider making a case to your manager as to who would be a more appropriate person to do the task.
- If the task is repetitive, look for ways to automate the actions. Consider completing it during low-energy times, delegating to someone who wants to learn, or putting a case to your manager for handling the task in a more effective way.
- If the task is truly pointless, share your thoughts with your manager but also remember to offer options and alternatives.
- If you still must do the task, try to break it into smaller actions. Consider each smaller action as a task in itself. Build the discipline to work through the tasks by interspersing them with more enjoyable tasks.

> Procrastination, focus and attention are all habits. Think of them as muscles: the more you work on them, the stronger and more dominant they become in your life. And the more influence they will have on your success and, of course, your productivity.

TAKING BACK TIME!

Paul was a "deadline junkie": nothing got finished until minutes before it was due. Once he worked out that he procrastinated due to feelings of overwhelm, he revised his approach to planning and completing his work. He built in milestones and set deadlines for himself that were days ahead of the actual deadlines. He also snuck in a few rewards for himself.

He calculated that his new approach allowed him to take back an average of one hour per day!

SOMETIMES A NEW JOB IS THE RIGHT ANSWER!

If you've done the work to understand why you are not as productive in your current role as you could or want to be, then determine if a new job is an option. Changing jobs can be stressful and it might not suit some. However, you will be more productive if you're the right person in the right job, at the right price and at the right place and time! Let me explain with a real example:

A woman called me once to say that I saved her marriage. At first, I didn't quite understand what she meant. She explained that following some coaching sessions her husband had with me, he took steps to go back to a previous role. In some eyes, that would be seen as a step backwards. But for him, he was going back to what he loved doing. He had more peace at home, reconnected with his wife and children and their budget was minimally affected. All they had to do was give up one bottle of wine and one night's takeaway meals a week to cover the financial difference! She was happy to have her husband back. Their health improved, too.

Changing jobs so you can do something you love is never giving up. It's not a failure. It's about boosting your productivity by reconnecting with what motivates you, what you're confident doing and what you're passionate about.

CHAPTER 7

SCHEDULING YOU

When I ask my audiences and clients to write down the five most important people in their lives, almost 95% of them write their partners, spouses, family members and friends. A few people write their own name but rarely do they write it first on the list.

Schedule you first! It's one of the hardest things to do, yet one of the most critical for achieving goals, boosting productivity and being healthy. It ensures you can deliver quality work to those who matter most to you.

Making yourself a priority in your daily routine is not selfish or self-indulgent. It's paramount to sustaining a high level of performance for the people and the tasks that matter.

Remember the oxygen mask concept in Chapter 1? In air travel, the safety message reinforces that you must put your own oxygen mask on first so that you are not in danger and can then help others. Scheduling you is your oxygen mask! It prevents burn out, helps reduce the negative effects of stress, keeps you focused and gives you the energy to achieve goals, be productive and help others.

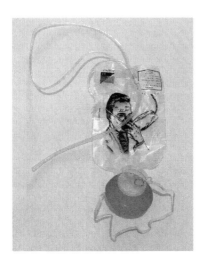

Scheduling you is not only about your physical health, either. It's also about your mental and emotional health. Psychologist Guy Winch is often quoted as saying, "We brush and floss but what daily activity do we do to maintain our psychological health?"

When you are at your most healthy, focused and energised, you can serve others to the standard you want and to the standard they deserve. But if you run on empty and continue to push yourself to serve others, then you are left depleted. You wonder if you truly gave your best. That is, you gave the best of what you had rather than what you could have given had you been at the top of your game.

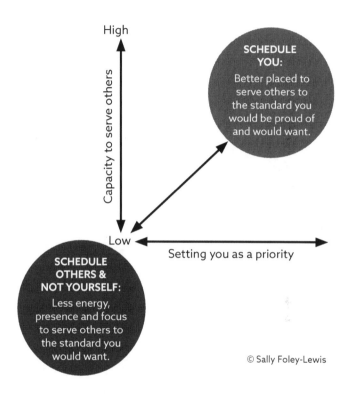

© Sally Foley-Lewis

When you are in the shower, on holidays, having a change of scenery or a rare late lie-in on a Sunday morning, do you notice that's when you have your best ideas? This is because you've done something about you, for you, and you've relaxed. Fine tuning the title of this book came while I was in the shower!

> *Previous book titles were a tad boring and I knew they were only working titles. I was pushing for the title but it wasn't until I changed scenery, relaxed, was in a nice hot shower that **ding**! The Productive Leader was the pick!*

Imagine you notice that a loved one always goes last and always serves others first. While at first glance it looks like they're being polite, you start to notice this loved one tends to miss out more than most. One day, this loved one confides to you that they are exhausted, depleted and burnt out. They tell you how much they care for others and love to help, yet sometimes it feels like it's never enough. You notice they even look depleted. What advice would you give your loved one? Most likely, you'd tell them to look after themselves.

A FEW SIMPLE WAYS TO START SCHEDULING YOU

1. Always aim to have a good night's sleep. Consider going to bed one hour earlier than usual, at least a few nights per week. This includes not looking at your device in bed. Read something light or fun rather than emails, reports or anything work related. Add a calendar reminder to switch off and go to bed.

2. Schedule all your breaks and self-caring activities in your calendar so they are allocated and you can

refresh. Use this time to walk outside, especially if you work in an office or environment with minimal natural light. Put up a private or out-of-office sign if need be. However, if you want to be an exceptional productive leader, you need to role model self-care. Let your people know that you are stepping out to go for a walk or some physical activity. It sends the message that self-care is important and influences the organisational culture of boosting personal productivity.

3. Schedule time in your weekly calendar to meal plan and shop. You are more likely to eat well if you set a meal plan for the week and prepare ahead of time. Even if you have ready-made or meal kits delivered, plan and schedule them.

4. Gratitude. There's a lot of research into the physical and psychological benefits of gratitude. Apart from thanking colleagues and employees as an easy and obvious way to improve relationships, showing and expressing gratitude for what and who you have in your life helps improve your wellbeing. Journalling each day by simply listing three to five things you're grateful for can improve your mental strength, resilience and self-esteem.

Your personal productivity is just that: personal. How you look after yourself, the way you approach your day-to-day, how you show up and be present for you, yourself and others matters. When you focus on what's most important in terms of achievement rather than being seen as busy; when you're able to physically and mentally go the distance; when you swap bad habits for helpful and healthy ones, your personal productivity rewards you. Your professional productivity and the productivity you get from your people are also positively influenced.

The productive leader is a role model of personal productivity for others.

IMPOSTER SYNDROME

- Do you chalk your success up to luck, timing or computer error?
- Do you believe, "If I can do it, anybody can"?
- Do you agonise over even the smallest flaws in your work?
- Are you crushed by constructive criticism, seeing it as evidence of your "ineptness"?
- When you do succeed, do you secretly feel as though you fooled them again?
- Do you worry that it's just a matter of time before you're "found out"?

If you answered yes to any of these, it may be a sign that you suffer from imposter syndrome. This can have a significant impact on your productivity. For more insight into imposter syndrome, check out the People and Management podcast with Dr Valerie Young:

Web: http://www.sallyfoleylewis.com/pm-39-imposter-syndrome-interview-with-expert-dr-valerie-young/

iTunes: https://itunes.apple.com/au/podcast/p-m-39-imposter-syndrome-interview-expert-dr-valerie/id905828790?i=1000374209324&mt=2

Stitcher: http://www.stitcher.com/podcast/people-management-with-sally-foleylewis/e/45906832

TAKING BACK TIME — AND ENERGY!

"The first time I started planning my day, it was a little awkward to be so focused on me. I think that's because I'd been focusing on everyone else's needs for so long. I would come into work and the first thing I would think was, 'What does such and such need? How far is so and so into the project? How much help do they need?' Never did I put me first. I didn't have any energy left after I'd taken care of everyone else, then when I'd get home it was my family's needs first. I may have squeezed in five minutes, locked in the bathroom, after 10.30 at night!

"All that has changed. I look after me first. The oxygen mask analogy really worked. I seem to have even more energy for others because I'd planned my day and got my priorities met. They're not hanging around me like a noose dragging me down.

"While I couldn't put an actual number on the time I've taken back, I know I have. I do more and I have so much more fun with my family on the weekends, doing so much more family activities."

— *Richard, Managing Director*

PLANNING IT ...
DECIDING IT ...
TALKING ABOUT IT ...
AND EVEN TALKING IT UP ...
ARE NOT THE SAME AS
DOING IT!

– SALLY FOLEY-LEWIS

PART 2

PROFESSIONAL PRODUCTIVITY

The productive leader takes care of their professional productivity; that is, their work, the tasks and projects they have responsibility for. They can confidently determine what the return on their effort is for any given activity.

When you are professionally productive, you lead yourself. By default, you are a role model for others. You inspire others to achieve top results from doing the most valuable work in the most effective way. Being successful at professional productivity means you are discerning and able to prioritise the important over the perceived urgent. You are the calm when all about you is a storm. You tackle tasks at the right time and at the right pace.

Key productivity strategies every productive leader implements include: batching similar tasks, time chunking to complete high-level thinking tasks, and avoiding multi-tasking to minimise error rates, save time and improve work quality. They control their day-to-day rather than letting the day and its demands control them. While at times circumstances and environmental factors can cause them to start chasing their tail, the productive leader can quickly identify when this is happening and take positive, effective steps to understand why, then shift towards working smarter and calmer.

To boost your professional productivity, start by answering the following questions:

1. What tasks and projects bring me the greatest returns?
   a) Returns for the organisation: that is, they are time and cost effective.
   b) For me: that is, for my development and enjoyment.
2. How would I group or batch my work tasks?
3. What usual interruptions do I face?
4. What part of my role do I hate doing? Why?
5. What part of my role do I love doing? Why?

CHAPTER 8

CLEARING YOUR SPACE FOR SUCCESS

CLEAR YOUR MIND TO BE MORE PRODUCTIVE

Clear the space so you can get the job done. When you have lots on your mind and you don't deal with those things, they will hinder your presence and productivity. The task at hand and the quality of your work will suffer.

The mind needs quiet. That's why it's so important to write down your feelings, thoughts and those niggling tasks that need to get done. Many of the suggestions researchers and studies put forward to calm the mind are not always practical or possible to do. Spending time with loved ones, hugging your pet ... they're great for clearing and calming the mind, but you can't exactly do them at work. Number one, think about the value of clearing your mind, and number two, think about the ways in which you do it.

Note taking is probably the easiest and fastest way to clear your mind when you're at work. Research by Mueller and Oppenheimer delved into the effectiveness of note taking, with interesting results. The study, published in *Psychological Science* (2016), found that writing notes, rather than typing notes, helped people process information more effectively. Recall is one element of this, but clearing your mind is another element.

If your mind is full of data and all your effort is going into trying to remember things, then you're not present. Your internal investment is low and you are unproductive. However, if you flip this around by making a small amount of effort to write notes, you actively remove the distraction from your mind. You capture your thoughts and "to-dos" so your mind can relax. This allows you to be more present, therefore you have a higher return on your investment, and that investment is your effort, your time and the outcome.

A "dump list" allows you to purge all those nagging thoughts and concerns, not necessarily the important stuff. Keep some Post-it notes, a notepad or journal handy to write everything down. Then, if you can, breathe, meditate or do some exercise before you get on with the task at hand. This will clear your head space and give you the boost you need for higher-level thinking.

I love Damon Brown's TED talk about writing on napkins. He talks about how US chemist Paul Lauterbur wrote his very first thoughts and sketches for magnetic resonance imaging on a napkin. Of course, Lauterbur went on to win a Nobel Prize for creating the MRI. And when rock star David Bowie was on tour, he penned his conceptualisation of Ziggy Stardust on a napkin. As Brown says, napkins are non-judgemental. That's what I like about clearing your mind by writing something down. It's not going to look back at you and judge you. It gives you clarity and helps you get rid of whatever's on your mind.

It's also a good idea to clear the space in a face-to-face context, such as when you have a meeting with someone. You can clear your mind by sharing the top three things that are going on for you. For example, once when I was coaching a client, I had just got off a phone call with a colleague after finding out we'd been given a publishing deal. At the beginning of the coaching session, I had to say to my client, "Let's clear the space. I need to tell you I just got off the phone from a publishing deal so that's pretty exciting!"

By sharing my news, by knowing it had been said I had "parked" it out of the way, so I could be more present with my client. I could give them more value. Consider sharing your "top three" at the beginning of a meeting, especially WIP (work-in-progress) meetings. You and your team will be more productive.

So, what's bugging you? What needs to be dealt with so you can get it out of your head?

CLEAR YOUR PHYSICAL SPACE TO BE MORE PRODUCTIVE

When you walk into your office or workspace and it's messy, what's your first impression?

If it excites you, gets you tapping into your creativity and innovative thinking and that's what you're paid to do, then step back and enjoy the scenery. Take note of the ideas and thoughts that emerge from the myriad papers, pictures, notes, articles, magazines and files lay strewn across your space.

Francis Bacon, renowned Irish-born artist, and Albert Einstein, the famous scientist, had cluttered spaces: Bacon an art studio and Einstein his office. Check out the images of Francis Bacon's art studio and Einstein's desk on Google! Such talent, inspiration and deep thinking all emerged from cluttered – or should that be rephrased as *creative* – workspaces.

Einstein is famously quoted as saying, "If a cluttered desk is a sign of a cluttered mind, of what, then, is an empty desk a sign?"

You may be in the situation where your desk is quite public and the organisation's expectation is to have a tidy, orderly workspace – irrespective of whether clutter boosts your creative thinking. If you work from home, do you feel embarrassed or anxious when clients or customers see your cluttered desk? The mantra *cluttered desk, cluttered mind* has been sung through many offices for many years. What truth is there to this? It depends on whether your workspace serves a specific purpose.

Psychological scientist Kathleen Vohs did a test to determine the effect of a clean or messy workspace. The result:

> Three experiments tested the novel hypotheses that orderly environments lead people toward tradition and convention, whereas disorderly environments encourage breaking with tradition and convention — and that both settings can alter preferences, choice and behaviour. Experiment 1 showed that relative to participants in a disorderly room, participants in an orderly room chose healthier snacks and donated more money. Experiment 2 showed that participants in a disorderly room were more creative than participants in an orderly room. Experiment 3 showed a predicted crossover effect: Participants in an orderly room preferred an option labelled as classic, but those in a disorderly room preferred an option labelled as new. Whereas prior research on physical settings has shown that orderly settings encourage better behaviour than disorderly ones, the current research tells a nuanced story of how different environments suit different outcomes.

*(https://www.scribd.com/document/158684501/
U-of-M-clean-desk-study)*

This puts a whole new spin on the adage that a *cluttered desk means a cluttered mind.* If one is orderly, tidy and decluttered in their workspace, it seems obvious that when they see a cluttered workspace, it triggers the impression of a cluttered mind.

In organisations that crave more creativity and innovation, it might pay to loosen any strangleholds in place on an orderly and tidy work environment. For a limited time or for the period of a project, consider nominating a space that can be left unkempt so the creatives in the team can do their best work.

If, however, you look at your workspace and it drains you because it is covered in papers, files, partly completed projects, new projects, old projects, mugs, plates and stationery, then now is the time to fix it. In her book *The Life-Changing Magic of Tidying Up,* Marie Kondo prescribes a massive clean-up that will not only re-create your space, but change your mindset about your space.

One viewpoint is that a cluttered space – a space where you avoid putting items away or let items pile up – could be a reflection of something else in your life piling up and not being dealt with. If this is the case, it's time to engage a coach or counsellor to help you deal with what's holding you in a cluttered state. This can lead into personal and deep aspects of your life, so individual attention is required. If this seems like you, invest in you and get yourself decluttered.

Meanwhile, start with the physical space. Here is a process you can follow:

1. BEFORE AND AFTER!

Take a photograph of your cluttered space. Capture how it looks now. Your "before" photo can be a strong motivator.

Think about how you would like your workspace to look when it is clean, tidy and inviting. Consider how you want others to think of you in your space. Your workspace impacts your personal brand. Here are some statements I have heard made about some offices and their occupants:

> *"He's a great guy but I hate going into his office in case I get lost and can't find my way out!"*

> *"I always book a meeting room for meetings with [her] because her office is so messy and dirty. She has used tissues and old coffee cups all over her desk. I feel like I'd catch something if I had to spend more than 30 seconds in there!"*

"Our building is old, cold and run down and it's hard to keep this place clean. I think that's why (he) doesn't even bother to try. No one likes going anywhere near his cubicle, it's revolting."

Do people think like this about your workspace? Step back from your desk or workspace and put on your "objective goggles": is it in need of some cleaning, decluttering … love?

2. DISCARD FIRST

Before you spend a lot of money on new storage containers, do the discarding first. You may find you don't need the containers after all. Items that are faulty or broken should be sent immediately for repair or be discarded. This may impact a depreciation register, so seek assistance to have that dealt with straight away.

Sort paperwork with a filter of disposal first, file second. A significant proportion of paperwork is stored as a file on a computer system. If this is so, discard the paper as per your company policy: recycle, shred, etc.

Any food or beverage-related items need to be removed for cleaning and stored back in the kitchen / staff room or be disposed of.

Bundle all the stationery into a pile and consider what you would realistically use. Think back over the past week. What stationery did you use? Return unused items to the stationery stores.

> In my first office job, I would take home my diary and a few files to work on or journal articles to read, and with that would come a pen. After a few months, I noticed I had a stack of pens at home – the first time I noticed I had 37 pens, to be exact! I took them back to work and popped them in the stationery cupboard. It was an eye opener for how the little things do stack up!

Knick-knacks, mementos and trinkets represent great memories of the good work you or your team has done, a special event, or a happy client who appreciates you. If you look at these daily and they give you a boost, keep them. Find a space for them that will constantly be in your line of sight. But if they are paperweights that hold no value, discard them. If you feel obliged to keep them, think about how they can be displayed in the office. Remember, though, you can value the moment, team or client without needing an object. A photo of the object may be a nice alternative to having the actual object cluttering your space.

Note: There will be items you keep and use in such a way that they simply won't stay organised and orderly. Stop expecting them to be orderly, find a container for them and move on.

Some files need to be stored for regulatory purposes. Your workspace is not the archive room! Put files in their proper place.

3. ONE DAY!

- *"The minute I throw this out, I'll find a use for it and need it!"*
- *"I kept this because I want to use it for a project I have in mind."*
- *"I've kept this journal because it's got a great article I want to read."*

If you've not used an item for more than three months or not read a six-month-old journal, you're not likely going to use it or read it. Throw it out or pass it on. By the time you have a use for ***that*** item, you'll discover a newer, better version. By the time ***that*** project emerges and becomes live, there'll be plenty of up-to-date data to rely on. By the time you set aside time to read ***that*** article, it'll probably be online.

> I have subscriptions to many journals. I don't read nearly as fast as they arrive, so I schedule time in my calendar specifically for journal reading. This ensures that I'm: 1) Keeping up to date with my professional development; 2) Not wasting money by subscribing and not reading; and 3) I can see the stack of journals shrinking rather than piling up and overwhelming me.

4. CLEAN

A significant amount of dust and dirt can gather on walls, under desks, behind cupboards and in drawers. You breathe that in daily. Clean keyboards and computer accessories in accordance with warranties and as suggested by the brand / maker. Pull out desks and cupboards from walls and thoroughly clean. Consider washing walls; it's surprising how much better walls look and the impact on the room when cleaned.

Empty the space rather than rummage through it. Empty draws, cupboard shelves and filing cabinets, then put back what you want. It's much easier to put the right items back in an empty space than it is to fumble through your items in a full or cluttered space as you decide what to eliminate.

5. RIGHT ITEMS IN RIGHT PLACES

It's time to re-create your workspace. Return the clean furniture and be mindful of every item you put back. Consider how often you use each item and if they really need to be in your space or could be stored elsewhere.

If you have drawers, use them. Put like with like. The same goes for paperwork you must keep on hand. Keep like with like: wages information should be together; monthly reporting should be together; and project information should be together. As noted already, if something doesn't seem to be organisable, then stop expecting it to be and be resolved with the most logical place you find for it. *(By the way, you're not allowed to be resolved with everything being on your desk! You get that, right?)*

If your office or space does not have a bin, buy one and have it next to your desk. This way, you can use it to discard immediately what you don't need.

6. PHOTO

Time to take the after shot!

7. KEEP IT DECLUTTERED

When you use something, put it back in its place. Give yourself permission to remain decluttered by telling yourself, "Everything has a place and everything in its place!" And: "If I put it back now, I know exactly where it is next time I need it." Don't cop out and dump "stuff" on the closest flat surface. Put it straight back when you've stopped using it.

Schedule in your calendar 10 minutes of tidy time once a week: add it to your calendar like it's one of your most profitable meetings/appointments. Make it a regular practice. If you do a quick 10-minute tidy up on a Friday afternoon, on Monday you will walk into a clean, tidy and orderly workspace that motivates you. Remember, the productive leader is a role model: if you make this a regular practice, it will be noticed by others and inspire them to follow your productive example.

TAKING BACK TIME!

"Once I cleaned out the spare room of everything not related to my business, cleaned the room thoroughly and then only put back what I needed, I felt lighter and more engaged with my business," Michelle said.

She added, "The amount of time I save by putting items back where I get them from, rather than just dumping them on a counter, chair or floor, might by tiny each time, but it does add up. It took time to embed this new habit but it has been totally worth it. I don't get frustrated looking for things because they are exactly where I left them, that is, where they should be."

LISTS: TO-DO, TO-DON'T, TO-DONE

The most popular list is the to-do list. If you already write a to-do list, that's great, unless looking at it overwhelms you. A to-do list is not helpful if it demotivates you. It should be a tool in your productivity toolkit, not a drag on your already busy mind and day.

Your to-do list is for one day, renewed daily. If your current to-do list has more than 6-9 items written on it, review it. Look at each task and if a task can be broken into smaller tasks, then the smaller tasks are what need to be captured in your list. The bigger tasks and projects can be captured in your monthly or quarterly plans.

If you prefer even more structure to your daily to-do list, set up the list in categories, such as:
1. Projects, 2. Personal, 3. People, 4. Pleasure.

The to-don't list is a great way to identify what you need to stop doing. To-don't lists help you be more productive by calling out the actions, habits, tasks or projects that don't serve you well.

A to-done list acknowledges your achievements. It is a brag list that can boost your motivation and remind you that you have done and achieved more than you may realise.

WHAT WORKS FOR ME

I don't see myself ás being a highly effective or fast reader. For a few years, I would buy books that would sit on my bookshelf. Alas, the osmosis of bookshelf to brain wasn't working.

I decided to start a to-done list to capture all the books I had read. I love the visual, so I have posted my to-done list on Pinterest. I don't include novels, only non-fiction.

Check it out here: https://www.pinterest.se/sallyfoleylewis/books-ive-read/

CHAPTER 9

EXTERNAL TIME WASTERS

You cannot live in a bubble and be free of interruptions and distractions, but you can teach people how to treat and respect you and your time. So, too, can you respect other people's time when you think about the interruptions you could be creating.

You can't have 100% interruption-free time, 100% of the time. You cannot fully eliminate the interruptions, distractions and time wasters that are not 100% in your control. You can, however, take effective action to minimise time wasters and their impact on you and your productivity.

A UC Irvine study in 2008 explored the cost of interruptions. The researchers found that while interruptions led to people speeding up their work to compensate for the interruption, this resulted in increased stress and frustration. Additionally, people spent an average of 11 minutes on a project before they were interrupted. Then it took 25 minutes (on average) to get back to the point where they were before the distraction.

The same UC Irvine study found that employees working in cubes were interrupted 29% more often than people in private offices.

A 2011 report by Ernst & Young found that although Australians were becoming more productive, time wasting continued to cost organisations $87 billion per year. The top three costs were unnecessary meetings, unimportant emails and social media.

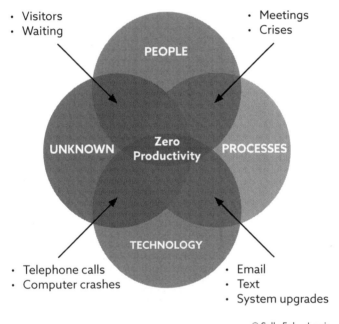

External Time Wasters.

External time wasters can be categorised into people, processes, technology and the unknown. It's like the game called whack-a-mole, where you have to hit the little mole that pops up. Every time you hit one, another pops up. Sometimes it feels as though the time wasters will never end, that there's an endless supply of "moles". The point is to:

1. Deal with them quickly and effectively.
2. Know it's not possible to be 100% rid of them.
3. Know it's about minimising as many as you can.
4. Then learn to live with the rest of them.

PEOPLE

You need the right people – people who refrain from interrupting others unnecessarily and can handle a certain level of interruption, given the nature of the work and the layout of the workspace.

At the Intersection of People and Processes:

External time wasters include unproductive, poorly facilitated meetings where actions aren't followed up or discussed.

When you think about some of the meetings you are expected to attend, do they start on time and end on time? Do they use an agenda? Meetings need to have some level of control and tracking. Nominate someone to be the productivity checker to make sure the meeting sticks to schedule, captures actions and allows the right balance of discussion. When business is completed, responsibilities should be assigned with follow-up dates to make sure the actions do happen.

Another time waster between people and processes is when someone doesn't follow a process and causes a crisis. For example, a workplace accident or poor workmanship.

> *When living in Abu Dhabi, working for a training company, our process was to check the exit hallways and bathroom of every venue we trained in. This was so we could be sure of a clear path and clean environment. Every so often, I'd find fire exits blocked by stacks of chairs or tables. If an alarm had sounded and we needed to exit, we'd find ourselves in a crisis.*

Many crises are avoidable. They occur because someone took a short cut or did something they shouldn't have, or because something was neglected. To minimise time-wasting crises, review past crises:

- What patterns emerge?
- What contingency plans do you have?
- What updates do you need to add to your contingency plans that will prevent a crisis reoccurring?

Some crises are beyond your control so, once through

it, understand why it happened and what you learnt from it. Explore what is likely to go wrong in the future, knowing what you now know. What triggers do you need to look for? Know what you will do about it in the future. Don't waste the lesson a crisis gives you.

PROCESSES

Without known and effective processes, uncertainty leads to frustration. If there's no clear way to complete simple processes, you will have multiple processes emerging for the same task. While this could lead to some innovative thinking, with tasks that are regulated and impacted by compliance measures, standardisation helps minimise time wasted.

At the Intersection of Processes and Technology:

Unexpected text messages and the continuous barrage of emails received throughout a "normal" day will only increase. Refer to the sections on batching and chunking in Chapter 12 so you can become more efficient at handling text messages and emails.

We all have our mobile device at work. In our breaks and even during our work time, we are prone to checking our phone for messages. In many organisations, there is a growing acceptance that employees use their devices for work purposes. What permissions do you give people when it comes to responding to text messages at work? What's the most effective way to handle your personal text messages?

System upgrades are generally known in advance. You are usually given notice that they will occur. Most are scheduled for after hours; however, this is not always possible. The key is to not waste more time while the system shuts down. Have a list of non-computer-related tasks you can tackle. These tasks could be reading journals – doing your own system upgrade! Schedule face-to-face or telephone meetings. Declutter your desk or your paper filing system. As frustrating as system upgrades can be, they are essential for crisis prevention. Use the time to tackle something else. Think of the time as a well-needed electronic break.

TECHNOLOGY

The love-hate relationship we have with technology seems to deepen daily. Technology has given us the world: it's connected us, taught us and given us modes of information dissemination like never before. We have become so reliant on technology that when something doesn't function as we expect it to, we react with heightened emotion and frustration.

At the Intersection of Technology and Unknown:

External time wasters include handling unexpected telephone calls and computer crashes.

Do you have the type of job that requires you to answer the phone, or are you able to trade time with this task? You may be able to ask someone else to take your calls for you or take messages on your behalf while you complete a task. Alternatively, let calls go to message bank, knowing that you can come back to them once the task is done. You can create a personal message on your phone such as, "I am currently focusing on an important task and will return all calls after X.00am/pm." Set yourself up for success. This includes managing others' expectations.

A computer crash is also at the intersection of unknown and technology, and is incredibly annoying. What you do in that time when a computer crashes could help calm the annoyance and help you get other work done, such as:

- Returning phone calls.
- Planning the rest of your day and week.
- Decluttering your paper files.
- Decluttering your desk.
  - The act of decluttering allows your mind to wander, which means ideas and solutions to problems can emerge. *(Similarly, ever noticed that when you're in the shower you suddenly have great ideas? It's because you're relaxed and not forcing ideas or solutions to emerge.)*
- Checking task and project progress with your people.

- Reading and catching up on the latest in your industry journals.

Don't get caught up in the frustration, complaints and disappointment that come with a computer crash. Use your processes and protocols to log the issue, then get on with other work. Use the down time to focus on other productivity-building activities, for example, building relationships, planning, reviewing goals and decluttering or clearing your space.

UNKNOWN

Given you cannot control all the external time wasters that can unexpectedly show up while you work, there will always be a certain level of unknown.

At the Intersection of Unknown and People:

Time wasters in this context include unexpected visitors. These could be external visitors to your organisation, such as customers, clients or stakeholders, or they could be internal people, such as workmates, direct reports, peers or senior leaders who turn up unannounced.

"Do you have five minutes to spare? Can I pick your brain?" This is a classic external time waster. While many do not intend to take more than five minutes, the reality is the conversation often takes much longer. Turning people away might feel career limiting, especially if they are senior leaders. However, if the relationship is strong, open and mutually respectful, you can politely and respectfully turn people away. But don't turn people away and leave it at that. Offer to follow up with them. Let them know you'll come to them in X amount of time or at a certain time. Reschedule it quickly so you can get on with what you're doing. Be sure to follow up – your reputation and credibility demand it.

Alternatively, ask someone to run interference for you. You can trade time with a colleague who will field questions or at least take messages on your behalf, and you can return the favour. Set a time limit and respect each other's time.

Don't be at your desk. Find an available meeting room or ask to use an empty office to complete the task. Put a notice on your desk saying, "I'm away working on a task. I'll be back here at X.00am/pm. Please leave me a note and I will follow up with you." Leave a note pad and pen next to your sign.

When it comes to stakeholders or external visitors, that is, your clients, customers and suppliers, you might not be in the position to turn them away. They might see that as bad customer service. Remember, these are the people who pay for your products or services, or provide you with supplies. You need them as much as they need you. Stop thinking of them as an interruption. Shift your mindset.

> *I was facilitating a productivity program for a group of high-level executive assistants and personal assistants, and we were discussing time wasters. One of the participants complained bitterly that she couldn't stand answering the phone. She hated it. "The phones keep interrupting what I'm doing." She was getting herself worked up just describing it. I asked the group what percentage of their job required that they answer the phone. The response was a resounding 80%– 90% of their role required they answer the phone for either one senior leader or on behalf of a management team. Many of the participants understood their role to include a level of reception, which meant being the person who answered the phones.*

> *My response to the participant's dislike of answering the phones was, "If answering the phone is 80 to 90% of your job, and you hate answering the phone, maybe you're in the wrong job." We all had a bit of a laugh, but the underlying reality was that she needed to come to terms with the fact that answering the phone was a significant part of her work. We discussed that she may be able to get someone else to periodically answer the phone on her behalf for short periods of time.*

> *This was a significant lightbulb moment for most of the participants, including the participant who in-*

itiated the discussion. Many mentioned to me that there were parts of their jobs they hated and they became frustrated and annoyed with having to do specific tasks. However, they realised their attitude made it worse. The mindset shift was critical to moving forward and finding ways to handle the tasks more effectively.

Here are some more tips for minimising the impact of external time wasters:

- Have reading material so you can read while you wait for people.
- Read and file, or answer emails while you wait.
- Return a call while you're waiting.
- If a meeting has a set start and finish time, stick to them: be there on time and leave on time, even if the meeting hasn't finished. You can suggest they reschedule a new meeting. You have been set an expectation, so stick to it. This is not about you taking the opportunity to score a point on someone. It is an opportunity to invite people to respect time. Prior to a meeting, you could set the expectation with a question, such as, "I see the meeting's finishing at 11.00am. I will leave at that time because that's how I'm planning my day." This may feel awkward at first, but if you do this and do it consistently, people will soon respect your process.
- Determine if you're needed for the meeting at all,

for all of it or part of it. Explore how much involvement is required of you.

- If you have an agenda item for a meeting, ask to go first. Be realistic and respectful of how much time your item will take. Stick to it. Leave when you're done and if you're no longer required in the meeting.
- If you run meetings, start them on time and finish on time!

OPEN-DOOR POLICY

Have you set yourself up to be a dumping ground? Many leaders tell their people that they have an open-door policy – that is, people can come and ask anything at any time. Even if you don't have the luxury of an office, no doubt you have been interrupted by, "Have you got a spare five minutes?", or "Can I ask you a quick question?" You may have even asked this yourself. It's never just or only five minutes!

This leads to people doing exactly that: asking anything at any time. This often becomes a noose around a leader's neck. On the one hand, you want to be seen to be open, available and accessible to your peers and team. But on the other hand, you want people to think for themselves, to problem solve and take some initiative before coming to you for direction on matters they should already know how to handle.

A frontline supervisor complained to me that he was sick of his team complaining to him, asking him about tasks and hiccups they should know how to do or fix. I asked him if he had ever told his team that they could come to him. He acknowledged that he had. His eyes widened and he exclaimed, "I'll never do that again." He realised he'd inadvertently created the problem.

It's not about permanently closing the door on an open-door policy; it's about how you handle people when they do come to you. New staff will need more direction and support. More established staff will need to be coached to think for themselves, believe in their own abilities, come up with the right solutions and do the right thing.

Asking is not in and of itself the problem. It's what it leads to if not handled well. What is your response when people ask you questions? The productivity gold lies in your reply. Do you give them the answer so that they need to come back and constantly ask you questions? Do you keep them dependent on you for direction? Or do you give a response that inspires them to think for themselves? This is explored further in Part 3: People Productivity.

IT'S NEVER **JUST** OR **ONLY** FIVE MINUTES!

– SALLY FOLEY-LEWIS

CHAPTER 10

MULTITASKING

If you'd like to drop your IQ by 15 points, multitask. According to one study conducted at the University of London, men who multitasked showed a drop in their IQ by 15 points – the equivalent of staying awake all night. Don't be alarmed, the IQ drop is temporary.

Multitasking is a myth. It doesn't help you. It makes you slower and contributes to errors and low-quality work. In fact, it's a time waster. According to David Strayer of the Applied Cognitive Laboratory at the University of Utah, 98% of people cannot truly effectively multitask. Only 2% of people show no deficit from multitasking. The two-percenters are called supertaskers.

Take football players as an example. The player with the ball needs to get that ball into the goal at the other end of the field. Halfway across the field, they don't suddenly stop, notice some rubbish that's drifted down from the stadium and pick it up. They don't stop and wave to the crowd. They are focused on one thing, one single goal, one single outcome. Others may attempt to thwart the player; however, they do not task switch mid-play. If they did, they'd soon find their contract voided.

The concept of multitasking is a false one. The reality is that you are not simultaneously doing two or more tasks: you are task switching.

The decrease in productivity when multitasking is caused by:

1. The time wasted switching between tasks.
2. The time taken to recall where you were up to with the task before switching.
3. Increased potential for errors due to switching.

Think about it. You not only need to pick up where you left off with one task and start moving it forward. You've also got to switch gears, go to yet another task and pick up where you left off with that one. The time, attention, focus and, therefore, energy and effort that go into all that switching is wasteful.

Multitasking is linked to interruptions and distractions. When you fail to manage and minimise these, you can easily be drawn into another task when you are mid-way through something else. Although that can be exciting and entertaining, you're not achieving – you're busy, and you'll need to use time and effort to return to the original task.

Each time you switch, it costs you time and energy. The cost may be minimal, but it builds over time. According to research cited by the American Psychological Association ("Multitasking: Switching costs", 2006), up to 40% of productivity is lost due to shifting between tasks. Imagine being asked to repay 40% of your pay. That's approximately two days of work per week. Unproductive!

When you task switch – that is, moving backwards and forwards, backwards and forwards though multiple tasks – you increase the chances of handling pieces of work more than once, work which otherwise would only have needed a few minutes of attention to be completely dealt with.

Stopping yourself from multitasking may not be easy, especially if you see yourself as part of the 2% who are supertaskers or if you are a high-sensation seeker or prone to distractions. Understand that it's virtually impossible to eliminate multitasking instantly. It requires making small steps.

Look at your work space. Identify the elements that are the biggest triggers of multitasking. For example, the phone (landline and mobile). Switch your mobile off or put it in silent mode for high-level thinking tasks. If possible, ask someone to take messages for you while you complete the task – eg. 45 minutes.

WHAT I LEARNT:

When I first switched my phone off to reduce distractions and multitasking, I was concerned I would miss an important call. I was worried that I could not be reached. What was really going on was I was worried that no one wanted me! At the end of the 45 minutes, I had missed zero calls! No one had called. Yes, it bruised my ego for a few minutes; however, I had completed my task and I was happy with the result. The whole experience taught me that, for small pockets of time, I can be unreachable for the higher purpose of productivity.

Let others know you need their help so that you can focus and be uninterrupted for a period of time. Let them know how long you need their help for, and ask if someone is prepared to run interference for you. Remember to return the favour.

Talk about multitasking with your peers and team. Discuss its effects and, as a collective, devise ways to minimise it. The topic shouldn't be raised to point out a personal weakness of any one person – rather, it should be raised for team discussion and reflection.

Bundle like tasks and tackle them together. This will move you towards a single focus rather than trying to switch between diverse tasks. This will be discussed further in Chapter 12.

Put your mobile device into airplane mode when driving, and do not disturb if you're using the map directions function. Also, be mindful that walking while looking down at your device means you might bump into people or posts. There is a growing number of cases of people being hit by traffic purely because they've not taken their eyes off their device.

Practice doing one activity at a time. Build this practice daily. For example, if you iron clothes while watching television, start separating the two activities. Time yourself as you do your normal load of ironing as a single task. Notice the difference in the time it takes and your sense of achievement.

The open-plan arrangement of modern offices has not been helpful for concentration nor productivity. It's an invitation for distraction and multitasking. If this is your office space, use a meeting room or ask to use an empty office to complete work that requires a high level of thinking.

If you are typing an email while talking on the phone, and the topic of the email and phone call are unrelated, there's a greater chance your email will be full of errors. Your ability to recall the phone conversation will also be hindered. Do one, then the other, not attempt both at the same time. It's also rude. If the person you're talking to can hear you typing in the background, it sends the message that they are not important enough for your full attention. Unless, of course, you are note taking and they know this. Stop typing and listen, or reschedule the phone call if your work is more urgent. Yes, this task switch will incur a time cost initially; however, it won't increase error rates, decrease quality or impact your recall. And so it will save you time later.

Multitasking can also cause you to gain weight! Have you ever mindlessly snacked on a packet of chips or lollies (candy) while working at your desk? If you're prone to snacking, then snack elsewhere. Enjoy the food, but not in your workspace. Your workspace is for work.

THE PERSON WHO CHASES TWO RABBITS, CATCHES NEITHER.

– CONFUCIUS

CHAPTER 11

URGENT VERSUS IMPORTANT

The mobile phone is no longer a phone first and foremost. Think about it. Compared to all the other features on your mobile device, the telephone component is often used least of all, right? Most people use their mobile to check their emails and Facebook before they get out of bed most mornings. Their phone is their alarm clock. And many people don't have a camera anymore – their phone is their camera.

We are plugged in, switched on and connected constantly. Whether this is a positive or a negative for you, only you can say. What is for sure is that we won't become less connected in our lifetime.

The impact of this ramped-up connectivity is the sense that everything is urgent. It's accessible now, so by default it must happen now, be available now, be downloaded now or uploaded now. What might feel urgent is usually created and "sold" to feel urgent, yet it has low importance when looked at in perspective to the rest of one's life.

And, as Stephen R. Covey of *The 7 Habits of High-*

ly Effective People fame said, "Most of us spend too much time on what is urgent and not enough time on what is important."

Bronnie Ware, a palliative care nurse who spent time with people in their last three to 12 weeks of life, asked her patients about their regrets. She wrote about their five main regrets in an article, which later became the book *The Top Five Regrets of the Dying.* The top five regrets were:

1. I wish I'd had the courage to live a life true to myself, not the life others expected of me.
2. I wish I hadn't worked so hard.
3. I wish I'd had the courage to express my feelings.
4. I wish I had stayed in touch with my friends.
5. I wish that I had let myself be happier.

Step back and look at your approach to your personal and professional life. Consider how you may treat some aspects as urgent *and* important, important, or just urgent.

What is important is seldom urgent, and what is urgent is seldom important.
– Dwight Eisenhower

The famous Eisenhower Box can help you determine what is urgent and what is important:

	URGENT	NOT URGENT
IMPORTANT	• Crises • Deadlines • Problems **Do it now!**	• Relationships • Long-term projects • Planning **Decide: This needs to be scheduled**
NOT IMPORTANT	• Interruptions • Meetings • Bookings (flights, rooms, etc.) • Answering certain emails or calls **Delegate: Who is best placed to handle this?**	• Wasting time on social media • Reading junk mail • Watching television **Delete: Eliminate or limit this**

Important tasks will give you long-term benefits and a greater sense of achievement. Put these high-value tasks first.

Considering the five main regrets discovered by Ware, reflect on what's most important to you. Review your work in the context of what is truly important and what is truly urgent. A legacy exercise is a valuable place to start:

1. Imagine you are retiring at the end of this week. Think about what you would like your closest work colleague to say in a speech at your farewell. Write down a few key points you wish they would say about you.

2. Next, imagine it's one month later. You've been gone for a month. What would you like people to say about you once you're gone? Write done a few key points.

3. Finally, using what you've written for steps one and two, plan what you will do to make those key points a reality.

Once you've done this, it should become clear what is important and what is urgent.

Can you ever get rid of the non-important urgent? No. However, you will have noted some strategies from Chapter 9: External Time Wasters that can help you minimise the impact. Delegation is an essential tool in the productive leader's toolbox, and is explored further in Chapter 16.

NOTHING IS SO FATIGUING AS THE ETERNAL HANGING ON OF AN UNCOMPLETED TASK.

– WILLIAM JAMES

CHAPTER 12

FOUR KEY PROFESSIONAL PRODUCTIVITY BOOSTERS

Two strategies that boost professional productivity are batching and chunking. Both contribute to task completion so that you achieve more success and have a greater sense of achievement. Emails and meetings are essential yet so frustrating in their volume and quality. Here are some insights and strategies to improve your productivity.

TASK BATCHING

Put simply, batching is doing like tasks in a set time frame. It's scheduling your work so that you complete similar tasks at the one time. This saves you time because you are not switching between a diverse range of tasks. Here's an example:

Schedule time to answer your emails three times per day. To do this, program three blocks of time in your calendar for emails – say, three 30-minute blocks. In these allocated times, you can read, file, delete and action your emails. Most email systems allow for an auto response to be set up, so you can inform people that you only answer emails three times per day and if someone needs something urgently they should telephone. You can copy and tweak these scripts if you wish:

I'm boosting my productivity by checking emails only three times per day. Be assured I will respond during my scheduled email time slot. If the matter is urgent, please phone me on xxxx xxx xxx.

Or

I check my emails X times per day, I will respond during this time. If the matter is urgent, please telephone my office / telephone me on xxxx xxx xxx.

Or

I check my emails at X:XXam, XX:XXam and XX:XXpm each day. I will repsond during these times. If the matter is urgent, please telephone my office / telephone me on xxxx xxx xxx.

What you batch will depend on the work you do: filing, cross-referencing, checking, processing, coaching, mentoring. You may already task batch and not realise it. If you've never batched tasks before, start with two similar tasks and get into a positive routine with them.

As you know, there may be interruptions along the way, but stick with it. Let others know what you are doing so they can support you.

TIME CHUNKING

This means doing a single task in the one chunk of time. Quite literally, time chunking is the opposite of multitasking. The success of chunking comes down to three key factors:

1. One single intention.
2. Distractions eliminated as best as possible.
3. Focus.

Like batching, you may already do this to some extent. The more you are aware of how you spend your time, the more you will value your time and spend it wisely.

Time chunking is an extremely effective strategy for getting through large pieces of work that require focus and high-level thinking. Writing a report, drafting a proposal, fixing a piece of equipment, performing surgery, preparing for a meeting or presentation are all examples single-focus activities that can be time chunked. I'm sure you'd want your surgeon to be single focused as they perform your surgery!

To set yourself up for success, block off a period of

time. You may want to follow the Pomodoro technique mentioned in Chapter 5. Remove all distractions by closing your email, diverting your phone and letting others know that you'd like to be left uninterrupted for that period of time.

Have only the relevant work in front of you so you can be single focused. State your intention, such as, "By the end of this 45-minute period, I will have completed this monthly report for the department." Set a timer and go to work!

When I first discovered time chunking, I had a cup of coffee and a small bowl of mixed nuts on my desk, along with the piece of work I intended to complete. Five minutes into the time chunk, I was fishing around in the nuts for my favourites and had lost focus! Solution: no more snacks while time chunking! Go to the bathroom before you start the time chunk and reconsider whether you really need that drink.

EMAILS

Emails were meant to be a productivity booster. They sped up communication so we could all save time, have instant access to attachments, communicate to multiple people at once, save money, save the world ... *all hail the mighty email* ... Well, maybe not quite save the world!

With all this in mind, the fascinating revelation is that you rarely hear people say how much they love emails. Yet in the same breath, you'll hear the same people defend emails as they provide them with proof of communication. Furthermore, you'll also hear those same people complain about the sheer number of emails and their detrimental effect on their organisation's lack of communication!

Does this sound familiar to you? Does any (or all) of this resonate with you? I hear these complaints regularly when I deliver productivity training.

The Radicati Group report for emails 2015 – 2019 stated that by 2019, we will be sending and receiving 246 billion emails per day worldwide ... *per day!* And by 2019, we will receive, on average, 126 business emails per day. To be productive, you must take back control of your email.

One of my clients asked me to mentor and train a manager who needed to improve his people skills and especially his communication. The manager's emails did not make sense and were considered too direct and aggressive. These emails were being sent to staff and external stakeholders. The business's reputation was at stake, not to mention the staff's morale. An audit of the manager's emails and process for handling emails concluded that the manager needed to:

- Slow down before typing, and especially before hitting the send button.
- Re-read emails to check for clarity and logic before sending, not just a spell check.
- Restrict each email to one key message, or at least separate topics with clear headings and spacing.
- Be reader focused: think about how the reader might perceive the email.
- Avoid ALL CAPS in general text, as it can be perceived as yelling.
- Think before jumping into the email conversation if the manager was only included in the email thread for information purposes.

Reports had been received that the manager's emails read as though he was inappropriately telling people how to do their job. In one instance, a client reported: "He's trying to tell me how to suck my own eggs." One unhappy client! This was not what the manager had intended. However, because he wasn't reader focused, his emails backfired.

Here are some tips for efficient email processing:

1. Don't be afraid to unsubscribe. If you've not read a subscribed email newsletter for more than three months, get rid of it. You're unlikely to go back and read them. Emails that languish in your inbox look like more work to do, which adds to feelings of overwhelm.

2. Use rules. Send important emails to different folders so you know where they are and can get to them later. You can use rules to delete email newsletters you feel obliged to stay subscribed to.

3. This comes out of David Allen's *Getting Things Done* philosophy of productivity: If you can handle an email in two minutes, do it. Get it done. Get it out of your way. If you can read it, action it and deal with it in two minutes, then you don't have to worry about it anymore.

> *Many leaders tell me they don't want to ignore emails or hold them over until the next day, even if the email arrives at 11pm. I wonder what the driving force behind that is. Is it about one's ego, their sense of being needed? Or is it about sticking to a brand and culture of always being switched on, of always being connected and attentive to your people and customers? Which one is it, ego or brand policy? Is this really productive?*

MEETINGS

The average meeting, without any travel involved, costs about $685. We attend on average two meetings per day. That's a lot of time spent in meetings. It's no wonder that 91% of people admit to daydreaming through meetings (sources include Verizon and Atlassian).

How productive are your meetings? Now, I'm not saying let's get rid of all meetings. Some meetings are incredibly important and they are a great way to disseminate information and have a decent discussion. But pay attention. Think about the hidden costs of meetings: getting the room set up, the agenda setting, the phone calls, the organisation and the cost of the people in the room.

Time spent in meetings costs money. It's a bit like a beautifully decorated layer cake. The outside icing is gorgeous and complete, and when you cut into it you see all the lovely, even layers. Meetings need to be like that layer cake: you must have the right ingredients in the right quantities, and you need to bake it properly.

For a meeting to work, you need:

- The right people in the room.
- The right amount of expertise participating and contributing.
- People to be engaged.
- To start and finish on time (don't overcook the meeting).
- To ensure business outcomes are captured and further actions assigned.
- To review whether the meeting is necessary as an ongoing medium for the group, team or task.

If you've got daydreamers in your meetings, make

sure your meetings are engaging. Meetings should respect every participant and not waste their time. Give participants responsibility within the meeting. For example:

- Time keeper
- Note taker
- Action note taker
- Chair / Facilitator
- Observer – if you're the one who usually runs the meetings, then ask for an observer who could give you feedback on your facilitation skills.

MEETING TIPS

To boost the productivity of your meetings, you may only need to make a slight variation to the way they are conducted. Get creative. Ask attendees for their ideas. Here are few to get you started:

- Have standing-only meetings (no chairs).
- Rotate meeting responsibilities.
- Run the meeting in reverse order – that is, start at the bottom of the agenda and work up.
- If pre-work is required, do not go over it in the meeting because one or a few people haven't done the pre-work. This disrespects those who did it.
- Start the meeting on time. Do not go back over items for latecomers.

- Warn meeting participants that there will be no admittance after the meeting starts.
- Start meetings at odd times – for example, 9.37am. It's a quirky pattern or habit breaker because it's not a standard meeting start time, such as 9.30am or 9.45am, people will take notice and will be more likely to arrive on time.

Let people know if you are implementing a new process in your meetings. Give them fair warning. This will set participants and your meeting up for success.

AN EMAIL IS NEVER URGENT!

– SALLY FOLEY-LEWIS

PART 3

PEOPLE PRODUCTIVITY

What's the collective value of everyone's effort? Your people are your greatest asset. People productivity requires you to encourage, build and sustain open and honest interpersonal communication to drive high performance. It involves influencing the right decisions and ensuring your team stays motivated and productive.

The productive leader actively builds rapport and increases the team's engagement through:

- Quality communication.
- Using delegation as a tool for development and not just task allocation.
- Providing timely and specific feedback. This means they do not avoid difficult conversations.
- Networking to deepen relationships.

People productivity relies on leaders to use their coaching and directing skills in the right balance for the right people. This means the leader must invest in each person to build trust.

To boost people productivity, start by answering the following questions:

1. How well does the team know me, *really* know me?
2. How well do I know each person in my team, *really* know them?
3. Do I know the ambitions, drivers and professional dreams of each member of my team?
4. What's missing from my interpersonal communication skills that will boost engagement and, therefore, productivity?
5. When was the last time we stopped to celebrate our successes or stopped for the sake of sharing a morning or afternoon break?

THE SIMPLE ACT OF PAYING
POSITIVE ATTENTION TO PEOPLE
HAS A GREAT DEAL TO DO WITH
PRODUCTIVITY.

– TOM PETERS

CHAPTER 13

KNOW THE STORIES,
SHARE YOUR STORIES

You cannot hate the person whose story you know!
– Scott Arbuthnot

When I first heard this quote, I knew I would never forget it. It serves a constant reminder for leaders to build better relationships.

This quote emphasises that the more you work to get to know your team, the better you'll understand them. You'll have a better insight into why they make the decisions they do and why they choose to do the things they do in the way they do them. It does not mean you will always agree with them, but understanding them fosters more trusting, open, honest and mutually respectful conversations. And together, you can problem solve more effectively.

If you don't take the time to build a relationship with your team, you cannot expect them to know or understand you, which can lead to a lack of trust and respect. Without a good level of rapport, your team won't know how you prefer to communicate. They will be left to assume. If you don't build a rapport with each member of your team, you will not know how to serve them as their leader. Sharing stories is one of the most effective, authentic and engaging ways to build relationships and trust. Sharing your experiences in a story, both work and personal, will give your team insight into you, remind them you're human, and invite them to engage with you.

In a 2014 engagement and organisational report collated by Tiny Pulse, the number-one reason why employees go the extra mile is camaraderie. *"My peers tend to be the best motivation."* This means the productive leader needs to look at cultural fit as well as skills when hiring. The productive leader needs to maintain a workplace that encourages and empowers peers to give each other support, recognition and that "pat on the back".

When a workplace is stressful and has a toxic culture, unplanned absenteeism increases. This results in losses to productivity, morale and product or service quality. Furthermore, unplanned absenteeism leads to increases in overtime costs, workloads and stress. With all these factors impacting on the organisation, this will inevitably lead to a loss of customers. The productive leader needs to address the issues that spark unplanned absenteeism and work with the employees to find workable solutions.

LISTEN

Listening is a fundamental communication skill that every productive leader must master.

Knowing what's going on with employees is important for productivity. Not only does it give you an insight into what works and why performance is where it's at, it also helps you address core issues rather than simply apply a Band-Aid to a bigger problem.

The act of listening, truly listening, shows employees they are valued. Taking the time to learn about them and to really hear their stories means you can understand what motivates them and what their values are so you can align their work with what they enjoy. When employees enjoy their work, they are more productive. By listening, you will enjoy your team more, you will be happier and you will enjoy coming to work, too!

SPEAKING UP

There are managers who claim that they engage their employees and listen when they have something to contribute. However, when you ask the employees if they agree with this, the story is often very different. If you want to know what's going on, listening is important, but you also need to ensure employees feel safe to speak up.

If you want your employees to speak up and let you know what's going on, be prepared to hear the bad, not just the good. If there is an issue, praise the employee for raising it. Do not shoot the messenger. You cannot fix what you don't know is broken, so being open to hearing from your team means they will not fear raising issues early. When an issue is kept hidden and its exposure and resolution delayed, it usually becomes a bigger and more expensive issue down the track.

TRUST

Aligned with listening and speaking up is trust. Your integrity and predictability in the eyes of your team foster your team's trust in you. If your team can rely on you to be where you say you'll be, to give equal consideration to everyone and every opportunity, to be fair across the board, to follow up when you say you will, it will go a long way to building trust.

Sharing your vulnerability and stories of your own lessons and learnings demonstrates that you trust your team enough to share the real you. When your team shares stories about themselves, respect them by not repeating those stories or using that information against them.

TO RECEIVE TRUST, YOU MUST FIRST BE TRUSTWORTHY

Lawrence was the managing director of a national company. During work hours, he was abrupt, aggressive and direct. One day he would fire someone for a minor issue and the next day give someone else a slap on the wrist for stealing company property.

Out of office hours and at work functions, he was soft, pleasant and chatty. It was quite disconcerting. He was neither predictable nor consistent in his integrity. He was feared by most and not respected by any. No one knew Lawrence's story and he certainly didn't want to know the employees' stories.

Lawrence didn't trust many people and openly admitted it, so no one trusted him. When asked how well he knew his team, he replied, "Enough to know if they are doing their job!" When the employees were asked about the culture of the organisation, one reply summed up their thoughts: "You don't have 21 people resign in nine months for no reason!"

TOOLS FOR KNOWING PEOPLE

There are many profiling tools and personality and behavioural assessments that can help you learn more about your team members. These provide structure within a soft-skills environment; an environment that is often challenging for managers.

A profiling tool gives a team a common language to better understand each other.

DiSC® is one of the most common assessment tools that profiles people according to behavioural traits. The quadrant-based model was based on the work of Dr William Moulton Marston (1893-1947) and examines the behaviour of individuals in their environment. It focuses on the styles and preferences of their behaviour.

The Belbin® Team Inventory identifies the diverse mix of behaviours people tend to adopt when working in a team. Dr Meredith Belbin devised the measure based on nine clusters of behaviour. This tool helps employees better understand how they perform as a team, and it's also helpful for project team formation and recruitment.

The Myers-Briggs Type Indicator® (MBTI®) is an inventory of psychological types as described by psychoanalyst Carl Jung. The MBTI® makes sense of the different types and helps individuals make sense of behavioural preferences.

Should you use a profiling tool? If you feel as though you do not know your team members well, you cannot determine why conflict arises, you sense a lack of engagement across the team, and your efforts to improve communication and your own engagement with the team aren't working as well as you had planned, then using a profiling tool may help initiate a renewed, improved strategy. The tools are not the answer – they are the beginning of, or a way to begin, better communication and workplace relationships.

FEEDBACK

Receiving feedback from peers, senior staff and your own direct reports is invaluable for determining how well you know and are connected to your team. Asking for feedback from those who report to you may feel awkward for you both, so every effort should be made to reassure them that you are willing to listen and that there will be no recourse if the feedback is well considered.

When in a feedback conversation, ask for specific feedback. If something is not clear, ask for clarification. When the person has finished giving you feedback, thank them. Sit with the feedback for a few minutes and reflect on what was said. If you agree with the feedback, start implementing change immediately. The impact of taking immediate action will send the message to the feedback giver that you listened and are willing to make changes. Others will notice this, too. There will be more on feedback in Chapter 17.

YOU MIGHT FIND PEOPLE ARE MORE PRODUCTIVE WHEN THEY'RE AT WORK IF THEY DON'T GO IN FEELING SO HASSLED AND STRETCHED OUT FOR TIME.

– NANCY KAYLOR

CHAPTER 14

CONFLICT

"No."
"I'm sorry."
"I don't know."
Three phrases that can boost your productivity.
– Unknown

Conflict is normal; it can even be helpful. Different experiences, backgrounds, values, perspectives and opinions can trigger conflicts. Seeing conflict as a dynamic part of your organisation can give you an edge in leading productive people. When conflict arises, it is often because your people care. They're invested and want to do well. If your people didn't care, they probably wouldn't bother to share opinions or perspectives that may differ from others. Changes to resources, processes and priorities can also trigger conflict.

Negative or destructive conflict is generally focused on people rather than tasks or required outcomes. When conflict is destructive and people-focused, you will hear anger and frustration, you will sense the tension increasing and the functioning of the group will decrease.

Here are some tips for managing destructive conflict:

- Immediately stop or call out behaviour that is directed towards a person rather than the task or outcome.

- Blaming and accusing will prolong the conflict, so shift the conversation towards understanding each person's point of view. Remind all involved that the key is to respectfully understand, which does not mean you must agree.

- Listen!

- Seek a common goal, even if that goal is to agree to listen and understand. Naming the intention is valuable for moving forward. For example, when you declare that the intention is to find a workable solution and, as the conversation continues, areas of difference start to cause tension, you can stop the conversation and go back to the point of intention. Consider it a "home base" to which you can return if destructive or negative conflict flares in the conversation.

- Ask for assistance from a neutral third party if the conflict cannot be resolved.

Conflict is constructive when, for example, discussion and debate generate creative and innovative approaches or solutions. In this positive conflict, the behaviours actively seek to keep negative conflict at bay by being task focused, non-personal and maintaining a positive – even fun – tension.

This type of conflict is beneficial when the focus is on finding the best solution. It becomes destructive when the focus is on personal tensions, personalities, egos or winning.

Effectively working through conflict can result in stronger working relationships. Handling conflict badly results in damaged relationships. It inhibits the expression of valuable differences in perspective.

The key to maintaining constructive conflict that is positive and task-focused is to ensure that everyone is clear about the intention. The intention is what you can return to should tension arise.

INTENTION

So often, misunderstandings turn into ugly conflict because the intention was not known, unclear or misread. If you state your intention before you act, others will have more clarity about why you take certain actions. This does not guarantee they will agree with those actions; however, you minimise significant conflict potential because your intent is known.

Conversely, asking someone else what their intention is can give you clarity and minimise potential destructive conflict. If an employee comes to you complaining about another employee, your first question could be:

- "Did you ask that employee what their intentions were?"

  Or:

- "Did you seek to understand what the employee was trying to achieve?"

THE SMALL STUFF – SWEAT IT!

The unproductive leader will diminish or make light of issues that hinder productivity, especially if those issues aren't considered important to the leader. What you consider minor may not be minor for your people. If these issues are not resolved, they will quickly shift from being small issues to significant ones that hinder morale and productivity.

An example of this was when a major national company began cost cutting and downsized real estate as its initial strategy. Staff wouldn't lose their jobs, but they would have to work at a new location. The biggest and most pressing issue for the company was saving jobs. The biggest and most pressing issue for staff was the travel to and from work and parking. While travel routes, transport and parking were not the responsibility of the company, these were issues that significantly impacted staff morale and led to productivity losses. Management did not listen, instead brushing the parking issue under the carpet with phrases such as:

- "We'll get to that, it's not important now."
- "You'll just have to get to work earlier to get a decent park."
- "Be grateful you still have a job!"

The management team's frustration over the physical relocation of an equipment-intensive business was evident. But its perceived indifference to the staff's issues resulted in communication breakdowns and arguments amongst staff and between management and staff.

Although the management team may not have felt it had the authority or capacity to solve the travel and parking issues, it could have put in the effort to listen to the staff and work with them to find solutions.

FRIENDSHIP OVER FUNCTION

The term "friendship over function" mentioned earlier in this book applies here, too. This is such a powerful reminder, especially in situations where values, perspectives and opinions differ often enough to maintain a rolling boil of conflict. Asking employees to respect the functions their colleagues perform helps shift the focus away from destructive – personal – conflict to the value of the work that's being done.

WHO EXACTLY SEEKS OUT A COACH? WINNERS!

– CHICAGO TRIBUNE

_____

CHAPTER 15

TELLING: THE MORE YOU TELL, THE MORE YOU REPEL

Telling, irrespective of the intention, often has a counter-intuitive impact on engagement and, therefore, slows attempts to boost productivity. On the other hand, asking builds engagement because it invites participation.

Coaching has a long history that can be traced to Socrates, who believed that individuals learn best when they have ownership of a situation and take some form of personal responsibility for the outcome.

© Sally Foley-Lewis

It's like being in a hailstorm versus a summer shower. A hail storm is damaging and leaves lasting dents. A summer shower invites you to play in puddles, gives life to the garden and can cool you down on a hot day.

By way of explanation, here's what happened to a leader I was working with. Renee was trying to engage her team in a new process to improve customer outcomes and build more capability across the team. The overall goal of the project was fantastic, the team even agreed it was a great idea, but no one put their hand up to do the work.

Once Renee had given the context and presented to the team how and what their action plan for implementation would be, I challenged her assumption of team engagement by asking: "Who had input into the project scope, desired outcome and creating the plan?" Renee's reply was that she had done it all. She was proud, and rightly so, for doing all the ground work. She had obviously put a lot of time and effort into the project to get to this point. Getting the project to move forward through her team, however, was looking impossible.

I helped Renee realise that what she had done was inadvertently exclude everyone from the opportunity to have input. While her intention was to save the team time and effort by preparing all the plans on their behalf, no one had any sense of ownership.

Therefore, no one was willing to put their hand up to participate. She had repelled the team.

A lot of time had been wasted because Renee needed to walk the project back to get the team on board. It was a valuable lesson because not only did she see that telling was repelling, once the team was on board with the project, they made significant suggestions that returned even greater outcomes.

If getting the team on board with a project has been near impossible for you in the past, ask yourself: how early or late have you invited them to take part and have ownership? Getting the team involved early is the key. Letting them contribute is the next step if you want them to be more productive.

TELLING KILLS THINKING

Have you ever felt as though you were left to do all the thinking? One of the most common complaints from managers is that they are constantly answering questions and sorting issues that should be handled by the staff.

One manager once said, "I should just take the door off its hinges, everyone keeps coming to me every five minutes to solve the smallest problems." The broader issue with this statement is that the staff have been invited to use the manager to do the thinking. If you tell your staff they can come to you any time, eventually they will. It's a double-edged sword: you want an open relationship, but you also want people to think and problem solve for themselves.

Here's another real example. In a group management coaching session, Mark grumbled that he was constantly interrupted by staff about matters they should already know. Mark's grumble set off a wave of like-grumbles from the group. This is a common issue. Leaders want to have an open-door policy, but the problem is the employees use it!

What Mark and many leaders do is give their staff the answers to their questions. They tell. In this context, telling has the opposite effect of repelling: it gives the asker permission to continually come to the leader and ask. A type of dependence develops where the asker doubts their knowledge. They lose confidence in themselves to decide or problem solve, so they turn to the leader for reassurance or an answer they already know.

To shift this, the productive leader invites the asker to think. The productive leader won't answer the question directly, but uses questions to encourage the asker to think for themselves. For example:

- Have you done that task or something similar before? If so, how did you start it?

- Has someone else done this task before you? If so, how did they start it? Or: Have you asked them how they handled the task?
- Where do you think the right information for completing this might be?
- Imagine you're giving someone else advice on how to do this task. What would be the first step you'd tell them to take? (And it can't be to go see the boss!)

Telling is a balancing act. Too much and it can be sticky or a repellent. In both contexts, the more you invite and ask questions, the greater the level of engagement, thinking and ownership.

A by-product of asking for input is the boost it gives to your team's confidence. They will learn to "back themselves" so they can get on with the work and even contribute further in more exciting ways.

TAKING BACK TIME!

"I seem to spend more small pockets of quality time with my team rather than many long, drawn-out and ineffective meetings."

Stephen started asking more and telling less. While there was a period of adjustment, the team really engaged with the change. This meant Stephen felt less drained and stressed each day.

When asked how much time he took back by shifting to asking rather than telling, Stephen couldn't put an exact amount on it, but he was adamant that he was spending a lot more time on work that was more aligned with his role and was more enjoyable. He did mention that there were four less project meetings happening per week, saving him at least four hours per week.

DECIDING WHAT NOT TO DO IS
AS IMPORTANT AS DECIDING
WHAT TO DO.

– JESSICA JACKLEY

SALLY FOLEY-LEWIS

CHAPTER 16

DELEGATION

Delegation is a tool for development, delight and de-stress! When you delegate properly, you can use it as a development tool for your team. It can lighten your workload and reduce stress. It's all about setting the delegation up for success.

According to a *Forbes* article by Martin Zwilling ("How To Delegate More Effectively In Your Business", 2013), London business school professor John Hunt found that only 30% of managers think they can delegate well, and of those, only one in three is considered a good delegator by his or her staff. This means approximately one manager in 10 knows how to empower staff through delegation.

In a 2014 Australian study, researchers Meagher and Wait found that there was a significant positive relationship between delegation and trust. Trust is fundamental to healthy relationships and relationships are fundamental to engagement and productivity.

Letting go and allowing your team members or employees to take on tasks and projects can be scary.

CHAPTER 16

Do any of the following statements sound familiar to you?

- I'll just check in to make sure no one fails.
- It's easier if I do it myself.
- They won't do it right.
- They won't do it to my standard.
- It'll take too long to show them.
- I've tried it before and it didn't work.

If yes, then know you are not alone. And know that if you keep using these excuses, you won't save time, develop others or reduce your stress levels.

Often, the root of these excuses is the manager's fear of failure. The consequences may also be high if the delegation doesn't work. Another common fear is that the employee is more skilled at the task or project than the manager, which leaves the manager feeling threatened. They become anxious about their job, credibility and reputation. Underlying these problems and fears is not having the right preparation and structure to delegate.

Delegation is like a remote control. Modern remotes have many buttons, but only a few buttons get used daily. This means the remote has untapped potential and value. Delegation is the same: when you successfully delegate, you give and receive far more value than you may initially realise.

This is my remote control.
It has 47 buttons – I use five!

Delegation provides advantages for you, your team or department and the organisation. These include:

- The organisation increases and improves its reputation as an employer of choice.
- When employees are given opportunities to develop and challenge themselves, their loyalty and productivity improve – or, at least, they do not decrease.
- When an organisation uses delegation to develop its employees, it is better placed to know who has

the competencies to take on higher duties. It can move people into roles more quickly and with less reliance on extensive recruitment processes.

- Employees' skills are developed and enhanced.
- Employee loyalty is strengthened as there are career-growth opportunities.
- The bottlenecking that decision making causes can be costly. This is a common problem with leaders who don't delegate. When staff are empowered to complete a task and make decisions, there's less waiting around for the manager to sign off. Things get done! And when things get done, the sense of achievement is increased, which improves motivation and job satisfaction.
- You have more time for strategic thinking and development opportunities.
- The work that has a higher return or value gets done.
- In your absence, the work will still be carried out.
- Your own reputation will improve: you will be seen and known as being a trusting leader who invests in the development of the team.
- Your career progression will be enhanced.

Be assured that when you do delegate, and when you do it successfully, you will have more time to do the higher-level work that is expected of your position. So often I hear, "But people might think that I'll be doing nothing." You will still have plenty of work to do, but it will be the right work for your role. You will be achieving more because, in addition to implementing the other strategies in this book, delegating creates more productive people, which allows you to be more productive.

Before you start delegating, you need to consider when and when not to delegate. Knowing when not to delegate is just as important as knowing when you can delegate.

When to Delegate:

- When it provides an opportunity to develop and train someone.
- When one of your people has a higher level of skill than you do.
- When it would offer an opportunity for one of your people to shine.
- When you have insufficient time and someone else has enough.
- When you wish to motivate and show confidence in someone.

When Not to Delegate:

- When a person is inexperienced or unskilled at certain tasks.
- When a person is unwilling to take responsibility for their own planning and productivity in a particular work area.

- When a person does not feel comfortable or confident in a particular task.
- When a person's performance, while satisfactory, is not outstanding.
- When a person is already at capacity – not based on an assumption, but after careful consideration and discussion.

There are three main parts to delegating: preparation, the conversation and the follow up.

1. PREPARATION

Determine *what* you can delegate. If you have a level of assigned authority to a certain task, such as financial decision-making and responsibility, then you cannot delegate that task to another person. Look back on your past two weeks and consider which tasks you performed yet know someone else could handle. Start creating a to-delegate list.

Ask your people if they are keen to take on any of these to-delegate tasks. Those who are keen will speak up. You may enjoy doing some tasks because you've always done them or you have put your hand up to do them, but this doesn't mean you should continue to do them. If the task is not relevant to your level of authority, consider putting it on the to-delegate list. Do your best to remove the emotion – besides, someone else might enjoy doing a task you dislike.

Choosing the right person to delegate to can be a challenge. *Who* can be tackled in two ways: task allocation or opportunity for development. If you have someone on your team skilled and willing to take on the task, by all means delegate. If you are in the enviable position of also having a few people who would gain professionally by learning how to tackle the task, then you could allocate the task to the person who is skilled and they could teach the others how to do it. This provides a leadership development opportunity for your skilled employee.

If you do not have a skilled and willing person, you need to establish how much you will need to train an unskilled yet willing employee.

Other considerations in your preparations to delegate include:

- Determine *why* you are delegating that task or project. Being clear on this helps you during the delegation conversation.
- What *resources* will the will person require?
- What *timeline* and *milestones* should be considered?
- How much decision-making *authority* and *responsibility* will the person need to effectively complete the task?
- Consider who needs to know that you're delegating the task. This will prevent people coming

to you, which may create a perception of "no confidence" in the person who is being delegated the task.

SLOW IS FAST!

All this and you still haven't delegated, yet! Yes, that's right. So often, managers dump tasks on people without enough thought or discussion. The employee is left to second-guess and make assumptions. They assume they've been given all the information, so if they don't understand something they hesitate to ask for fear they'll look incompetent. That's where everything starts to go wrong. The extra time preparing to delegate, and it takes less than 20 minutes of thinking time, will lead to much better results that reflect positively on you.

2. THE CONVERSATION

There are five key parts to the delegation conversation. Cover them all to ensure success.

1. **Explain the Assignment**
    Give all the details appropriate for the employee. Be sure to state the importance of the task and the *why* behind the task. Also, discuss your expectations in terms of standards and what a successful outcome or completion means to you.

2. Test Understanding

Use questions to check the employee's understanding of the task. You might want to use a question such as, "What other information do you need to start?" Or, "So I know I've not missed anything out, what do you understand about the project and how to move forward?" These are much better than, "Do you understand?", which can be patronising and really ineffective for the purpose of testing understanding.

3. Identify Problems / Gaps

Discuss – make it a two-way conversation – the potential problems, roadblocks and gaps that could thwart the task's completion. Ask the employee what might hinder their success, and listen so you can problem solve together.

4. Set Milestones

Avoid micro-managing and over-supervising by discussing and setting progress milestones. Agree on how progress will be reported. Ask the employee to tell you how they would like to be held accountable.

5. Summarise

Ask the employee to summarise their understanding of the task, the problem-solving strategies and progress-reporting schedule.

Finish the conversation by asking how the person feels about taking on the task, and how you feel about their ability to do it.

It might seem obvious to you, but it may not be clear to your employee that they can come to you if they get stuck or feel unsure. Be explicit about how they can approach you to ensure they don't procrastinate due to fear of failure or mistakes.

3. THE FOLLOW UP

Stick to what you have agreed to with your employee! The follow up is as essential as every other step in the process. When you don't follow up, it sends the message that the task and the person are not valued or important.

So often, disengaged employees say, "Why should I bother? The boss never asks or checks." Following up is not a difficult thing to do: schedule it in your calendar and treat it as you would your other important appointments.

TAKING BACK TIME!

Jeff had been told by his boss to delegate more. He hesitated, as he had tried to delegate tasks and projects to some of his team before, but it never seemed to go particularly well. With the amount of time Jeff spent chasing up loose ends, repeating his instructions and directions and being let down, delegation left a bitter taste in his mouth. He felt frustrated and doubted his own skills.

Once Jeff put his delegating process under the microscope and discovered where he needed to tweak the process, he stepped up and started delegating again. To his own delight, the outcome was better than he expected. Sure, he had a few hiccups here and there, but these were easily fixed and there were none of the dramas like he had previously experienced.

He discovered that by working closely with two team members for a few days while handing over a major piece of work, he easily took back three to four hours a week.

DON'T UNDERESTIMATE THE VALUE OF FOLLOWING UP!

Some years, six months could pass before the managing director of the company visited the branch office. During his rare visits, he was authoritarian in what he wanted his sales staff to do. He would draw diagrams all over the white board and talk about targets and how the company would suffer if quality and sales diminished.

He would then have a closed-door meeting with the office manager to berate him about the sales team not achieving what he had wanted them to achieve since his previous visit.

Once he had said what he wanted to say, he would travel back to head office and the team wouldn't hear from him for weeks, sometimes months. Not even a whisper. Specifically, no one would hear from him about any of the directions and actions he had commanded during his branch office visit.

While everyone would have preferred the managing director to be far less aggressive with his communication, the other critical reasons why no one would act on his commands were obvious: He didn't encourage or empower the staff to own the actions he wanted them to take. He didn't encourage the sales team to set clear actions, let alone provide clear directions on how to achieve his demands. And he didn't set deadlines with (or for) the sales team. In his meeting with the office manager, he neglected to brief him on what he actually wanted done. He didn't tell the sales team or office manager that he would follow-up with them. And he never did follow up!

As soon as the managing director left, everyone would spend at least an hour debriefing – whingeing, gossiping and complaining – about his visit, then go straight back to what they were doing before his visit.

Even if the managing director's style stayed the same, he would probably have got better results if he had regularly followed up with the sales team and the office manager.

I THINK IT'S VERY IMPORTANT TO HAVE A FEEDBACK LOOP, WHERE YOU'RE CONSTANTLY THINKING ABOUT WHAT YOU'VE DONE AND HOW YOU COULD BE DOING IT BETTER.

– ELON MUSK

CHAPTER 17

FEEDBACK

Examine what is said and not who speaks.
– African proverb

Feedback is information for change. Most feedback managers give (or are expected to give) is intended to bring about change: improved performance, productivity, amended processes or opportunities to value-add. Giving feedback without a change component is just giving information.

According to research by US professional services firm Zenger Folkman in 2014, 57% of respondents preferred feedback that was designed to correct behaviour versus 43% who preferred praise. Additionally, 72% stated they would prefer to receive feedback that provided corrective guidance.

Feedback, be it corrective or praise, needs to build confidence in the individual and the team.

One common complaint employees have is that they do not get any feedback that tells them how well they are doing or where and how they can improve. This lack of feedback (quality or quantity) leads to employees being disengaged in the workplace. And that means employees are not bringing their A-game to work. Their productivity suffers because they have no direction. While you can improve the way you give feedback to your people, also consider how you can improve the way you receive feedback from your employees, peers and senior leaders.

SKILLS FOR SUCCESSFUL FEEDBACK

Aim to give and receive feedback so that everyone participating in the conversation has a positive experience – even in the difficult corrective conversations. It's much better for positive and productive working relationships when the feedback conversation focuses on the problem or behaviour, not the person. A solutions-focused attitude and approach work best.

There are many skills that help create successful feedback conversations:

1. LISTENING

When you listen carefully, you demonstrate respect and concern for the other person. This will encourage that person to feel comfortable enough to contribute further to the conversation.

Listening allows you to detect possible reasons why

performance has slipped or why mistakes have been made so you can guide the conversation to resolutions. It's not an opportunity to find out who to blame and shame. Be careful not to get caught up in that unhelpful negativity.

Listening will give you clues as to what you can do to improve processes, systems and relationships.

2. ASKING QUALITY QUESTIONS

Asking quality questions goes hand in hand with gathering quality information. Ask questions that will encourage the conversation to flow. These are generally open questions that start with how and what.

Examples of questions that encourage a conversation to flow:

- What specifically has been the biggest challenge to completing the task?
- How can you streamline the process?
- What short-term support do you need to complete the project?

The person who asks the question controls the conversation. This means you can direct the conversation with a question. It also means you will do less talking and more listening. I'll repeat that: you will do *less talking* and *more listening*!

Here are some tips for asking quality questions that result in greater engagement and results:

1. One Question at a Time

Ask only one question at a time. I'm sure you've observed a situation, even been on the receiving end, where one person has started to ask a question, then went on to explain why they were asking the question, then went on to give more background detail, then went on to practically answer the question, then went on, and on, and on …

While well intended, what happens is that the real question is never properly asked and an answer is never properly sought or provided.

Ask one question, then listen. Sounds simple enough, yet it's not always easy to do. It may take practice.

2. Silence is a Valuable Tool

Use silence. When a question is asked, sometimes the response is an immediate, "I don't know," or a period of silence. Avoid jumping in to fill the silence. Let the person think. Give them the space and silence to reply. This shows the person you're prepared to wait for an answer. If you must speak, encourage the person to think about your question as if they did know the answer. Ask what their initial thoughts are.

3. ADAPTABILITY AND FLEXIBILITY

Being adaptable and flexible is about taking the conversation where it needs to go. Be prepared to go back and forth if the actions discussed and initially agreed upon don't gain commitment. Give yourself and the person time to have an effective conversation without feeling rushed. This means productive and positive outcomes will be achieved sooner rather than later (and after repeated unsuccessful feedback attempts).

4. PROBLEM SOLVING

It's important to find ways to help the person do their own problem solving. Avoid giving them the answers straight way. Even if you know the "right" answer, stop! Let the person think. Don't cave into the pressure to speed through the conversation.

Problem-solving skills involve identifying what the real problem is and breaking it down into manageable chunks. You may already understand the problem and how to solve it; however, better, longer-lasting results are achieved when you encourage the employee to work out and suggest actions for change. You can do this by asking quality questions that encourage the employee to think the problem through.

If the employee struggles to think of potential solutions, then you can provide prompts or suggestions. If you must give suggestions, give three so that the employee must choose. The aim is for the employee to have as much ownership over the actions as possible.

Consider these skills as the foundation of successful feedback conversations. If you struggle to see the value in them, think of how skilled you'd like a person to be if you were on the receiving end of feedback.

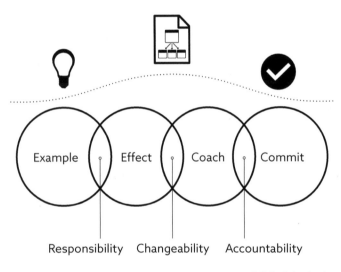

© Sally Foley-Lewis

Feedback Formula.

248 | SALLY FOLEY-LEWIS

The formula can be explained this way:

INSIGHT	ACTION PLAN	ACHIEVEMENT
By stating or showing the person what the feedback is (eg. evidence) and discussing the effect the current situation has on work output, quality, the team, resources, profits, etc., you create insight for the employee. This, in turn, helps the employee feel a greater responsibility to act.	Having a greater sense of responsibility to make change – eg. improvements, amendments, value-adding – means the employee will have an increased willingness to step in and create an action plan. Their performance is more likely to change for the better.	By coaching the employee to create their own action plan for change based on the feedback and gaining their commitment, as well as demonstrating your own commitment to support the employee, you create an accountability that will lead to achievement.
RESPONSIBILITY	CHANGEABILITY	ACCOUNTABILITY

GIVING PRAISE

Example:
- Provide a specific example of the person's good work so they can clearly link their actions to the feedback.
- Be specific. Thank them. The more specific you are, the better the person can relate to the task and their own positive or helpful behaviour.

Effect:
- Provide the person with insight into the benefits (effects) gained from their actions.
- Explain the effect of the person's behaviour. This means you will be answering any questions the person may have about why you are highlighting their behaviour. You are answering the person's "so what?"
- Describe the benefits to the individual, team, organisation, budget, profits, reputation, etc.

Coach:
- Facilitate (not direct or dictate) a discussion about how the person's actions can be continued, shared or applied in other areas.
- Encourage them to implement an action plan.
- If no further action is needed or can be taken, simply (yet importantly) thank the person for their efforts.

Commit:
- Establish commitment to embed the actions for results and success.
- Ensure commitment by:
  - Setting and sticking to follow-up dates.
  - Asking the employee how they would like you to help them be accountable.

Not everyone likes to be praised or acknowledged in public, so be mindful of the person and how they might prefer to be praised. Give praise as soon as possible after the event.

Here are some examples of how you can give effective praise and feedback:

EXAMPLE NO. 1

Example: I want to take a minute to discuss how pleased I am that you took the initiative to review and streamline the job-sheet process.

Effect: Since you did that, I've noticed a much quicker turnaround in reporting the completions to the customer relations department. I'm also tracking to see if there have been other savings, such as job completion times.

Coach: You've got great initiative. Is there any other area you are keen to review or is there anything else in the job-sheet process you think can be further developed?

(Allow discussion: ask quality questions and listen.)

Commit: I want to close our conversation by again saying thank you, and letting you know I'm committed to supporting you with the next project. I want to check how committed you are to keep going.

(Note: Leave the conversation on a good note. Encourage the person to have the last say about the feedback, such as how they feel about the next steps discussed during the coach step.)

EXAMPLE NO. 2

Example: You did a brilliant job of getting the project finished ahead of schedule, particularly driving the team while keeping morale up and costs down.

Effect: This has given us a 10% buffer in the budget and almost three months' wiggle room on the other two projects. I can tell you the rest of the teams will be mightily impressed! The board has also been made aware and is looking for a way to recognise you for what you've done. Are you okay about some public acknowledgment and recognition?

Coach: I'm keen to know your thoughts on what

you did in the project that could be done on other project sites.

(Allow discussion: ask quality questions and listen.)

Is this something you would like to continue with? How would that look like for you operationally?

Commit: I want to close our conversation by again saying thank you. I really am very pleased and thank you for all your effort. Lastly, please rest assured that I'll support you in the implementation. Now, can I check with you how committed you are to seeing this continue?

(Note: Leave the conversation on a good note. Encourage the person to have the last say about the feedback, such as how they feel about the next steps discussed during the coach step.)

EXAMPLE NO. 3

Example: The sales figures are in and you had a brilliant month, thank you. I noticed in your plan you had set a 5% increase, yet pulled in 9.75%. Well done! You must be pleased with yourself, as you should be.

Effect: This is an awesome result and will give the team a real motivational boost. Given we are also talking about how tough the market and economy are, this will show the team that exceeding expectations can be done.

Coach: What was it about your approach or your efforts that made the difference this month?

(Allow discussion: aim to learn about possible strategies that can be replicated or shared across other areas and/or with other staff. Ask quality questions and listen.)

Would you be keen to share some of these actions with the team?

Or

How can we share these actions or tips with the rest of the team?

Or

How can these results be continued?

(Allow discussion: ask quality questions and listen.)

Commit: Again, thank you for your good work and great sales figures. Let me know how I can help you keep this up. I want you to have the support you need.

(Note: Leave the conversation on a good note. Encourage the person to have the last say about the feedback, such as how they feel about the next steps discussed during the coach step.)

CORRECTIVE FEEDBACK

Example:
• Provide a specific example of the negative, incorrect or damaging behaviour/s or action/s so the person can clearly recall it and link to what you're saying.
• The more specific you are, the better.

Effect:
• Give a clear explanation of the effect of the person's behaviour, such as the impact it has on the team, organisation, budget, safety, project success, future opportunities, etc.
• This will give the person a reason as to why their behaviour was incorrect. Explaining the effect answers their "so what?"

Note: There may be valid reasons for the behaviour that need to be addressed. These reasons could include the person not knowing the proper process, not being kept up to date on procedural changes or not having the skills to do the task.

The amount of time the work has been impacted by these reasons will also need to be addressed. Focus the discussion on understanding when the problem or behaviour occurred. Do not blame anyone. When you blame, you create a roadblock to overcoming the issue because people will naturally become defensive. Encourage the employee to avoid blaming others.

Coach:
- Lead the discussion about what changes the employee can and will make.
- Coach, rather than direct or dictate, the employee to identify actions for change.
- The more the employee is engaged, empowered and enthused to identify actions for change, the greater they will own the process – and the better the chances of positive change occurring.

Commit:
- Establish commitment to embed the actions for results and success.
- Address commitment in two ways:
  1. Them: End the conversation by getting them to commit to the new behaviour.
  2. You: Assure the person you are committed to helping them. Ask them how they would like you to support them and keep them accountable.
- Set follow-up dates and times and stick to them!

Corrective feedback is valuable only when it is clearly understood, when actions for change are identified and when there is commitment.

EXAMPLE NO. 1

Example: I want to bring to your attention the required weekly work (specifically state what the work is) for XYZ client and ABC client. It hasn't been completed for the past three weeks.

(Be specific so the person can make the link.)

Effect: By not completing the weekly work, we cannot achieve the results for our clients, which they expect and pay us for. When the work is not done, the client has a right to not pay us and that directly impacts our cash flow, profits and ability to operate.

What has happened in the past three weeks that has caused the work to not be completed?

(Allow discussion: ask quality questions and listen.)

Coach: What can you do to turn this situation around?

Or

You can appreciate this work needs to be done regularly. Our clients directly rely on regular input. What actions can you take today to catch up?

Or

How can we fix the problem and move this forward so the work can be done weekly and not fall behind?

(Allow discussion: ask quality questions and listen.)

(Note: Create a plan of action with the person. Encourage the person to develop action steps so they have complete ownership of the plan.)

Commit: I want to close our conversation by encouraging you to get on top of this work. I think you've got a good plan now to get back up to speed. I'm committed to supporting you with this, so please come to me if there are any hiccups along the way. I want us to have a quick five-minute catch up this Friday at 9am just to make sure all is on track. How committed are you to getting on with this work now?

(Note: Leave the conversation on a good note. Encourage the person to have the last say about the feedback, such as how committed they feel about the next steps discussed during the coach step.)

EXAMPLE NO. 2

Example: I want to bring to your attention your late arrival to work recently. I've noticed you arrived at 9.15am last Monday, 9.20am on Tuesday, 9.45am on Thursday and today at 9.20am.

(Be specific so the person can make the link.)

(Note: Vague examples such as "late this week" will not provide a strong enough reference point for the employee. The more specific the example, the better able the employee will be to connect with the behaviour. There will also be less chance of the employee finding flimsy excuses or brushing the feedback off as weak because there isn't enough evidence.)

Effect: I'm not sure if you're aware of the impact your late arrivals have had on others. For example, one staff member needed to reschedule a client meeting because they couldn't leave the office unattended. While it's not life and death, it does impact our client relationships. We don't want to mess clients about or lose clients. I also wanted to chat with you on Tuesday morning about Mr Smith's account before I met with him and you weren't here for me to do that. I wanted to get as much information about the account as possible. With you not here, I wasn't fully prepared. This left me concerned that our company didn't look professional.

What's happening to cause the recent lateness?

(Allow discussion: ask quality questions and listen.)

(Note: There may be valid reasons that need to be addressed. Focus the discussion on understanding the underlying reason why the person has been late. Avoid any direct blame.)

Are you aware of the policy about hours of work and lateness?

(Explain the policy or remind them of it.)

Coach: What do you need to do to arrive on time or cover the time you miss by being late?

Or

How can you turn this situation around? What can I do to help you get back on track?

(Encourage the person to problem solve rather than you direct them. Ask quality questions and listen.)

(Note: Create a plan of action with the person. Encourage them to develop the action steps so they have complete ownership of the plan.)

Commit: Thank you for being honest and open about the situation. I know you are normally a good time manager so I want you to know I am here to support you as best I can. How committed are you to turning this around?

(Note: Leave the conversation on a good note. Encourage the person to have the last say about the feedback, such as how committed they feel about the next steps discussed during the coach step.)

EXAMPLE NO. 3

Example: I want to have a chat with you about the monthly reports you've been submitting. You may have noticed that for the past four months, the reports have been returned to you with many more corrections required. (Have copies on hand and show the employee). We all make mistakes. I'm just noticing a bit of a difference in quality these past few months.

Effect: Because of the extra time needed to make the corrections, the reporting is being held up at the GM's office, which gives his office less time to prepare their reports for the board. There is a clear knock-on effect.

Prior to these past four months, everything was fine. What's going on for you?"

(Allow discussion: ask quality questions and listen.)

(Note: There may be valid reasons, which need to be addressed. Focus the discussion on understanding the underlying reason why the person's work standard has slipped. Avoid any direct blame.)

Coach: What help do you need to get the reports back to standard?

Or

What other work can you delegate, even temporarily, so you can catch up?

(Allow discussion by encouraging the employee to problem solve. Ask quality questions and listen.)

(Note: Create a plan of action with the person. Encourage them to develop the action steps so they have ownership of the plan.)

Commit: I'm glad we talked about this. Your work is normally really good and I wanted to make sure everything was okay with you. Thank you for helping problem solve this and finding a way forward. I am here to support you as best I can. Out of a score of 10 (10 being the most), how committed are you to putting this plan into action?

(Note: Leave the conversation on a good note. Encourage the person to have the last say about the feedback, such as how committed they feel about the next steps discussed during the coach step.)

Unlike praise, where it may be suitable to provide feedback in a public setting, that is not the case for corrective feedback. Given that this type of feedback is focused on an action or behaviour that needs to improve or change, it is most appropriate to meet in private so the person doesn't feel embarrassed or humiliated by others listening in or observing.

Give corrective feedback as soon as possible after the event occurs or after you notice a change in behaviour or performance standards. Give corrective feedback at a time when you and the person aren't rushed or distracted.

Storing corrective feedback for the formal annual performance review is unfair to the person. It means they will have to remember their actions from up to a year ago. Could you remember what you did a year ago? If you don't address poor performance or mistakes as soon as possible, the negative impact on productivity, resources, relationships and finances will be prolonged.

When corrective feedback is dealt with, and performance is back to the right standard, avoid focusing on it or reminding the person about it. Let it go. At the time of an annual performance review, it would be a positive gesture to praise the extra effort the person put in to get back to the right standard of performance.

If the performance does not improve, you may need

to escalate the issue to a disciplinary process. Be clear, consistent and follow your performance management or disciplinary policies to help the employee improve or to be removed. Check your local laws about employment termination so you can be assured of following the right steps. In Australia, check out Fair Work Australia: www.fairworkhelp.com.au or the Fair Work Ombudsman: www.fairwork.gov.au

THINGS TO AVOID WITH PRAISE AND CORRECTIVE FEEDBACK

Avoid insincere, vague and irrelevant feedback. Statements such as "great job" without a reference to a particular task will not provide enough of a direct link for the employee to know exactly what they did well.

Praise boosts the ego and nurtures confidence. You do not need to go overboard. Be specific and show you sincerely value the work they have done.

Statistics show that employees want to know whether they are doing a good job. They want to know what's expected of them and where they can improve. This requires you to give feedback. Use the example, effect, coach and commit steps to ensure you have a structured and complete feedback conversation.

Some leaders believe giving praise diminishes their power or authority. They are quick to criticise and never give praise. The working relationships in these environments are often strained, with employees not feeling at ease at their work. This impacts productivity as staff do the minimum amount of work possible. They expend their energy on avoiding criticism rather than on more positive and productive pursuits, such as bringing innovation and creativity to their work.

Avoid ego getting in the way of genuinely positive, open and honest working relationships. This is not about getting deeply personal or making everyone your best friend. It is about building relationships so your people feel safe to try new things without constant criticism.

RECEIVING FEEDBACK

Just as it is your role to provide feedback, you also need to be able to receive it. Your own productivity can improve by asking for and receiving feedback. Feedback from your employees, peers and senior leaders is invaluable for gaining greater insights into your leadership. When asking your employees or direct reports for feedback, it must be done with an assurance that they are safe to provide the feedback.

The more specific your questions, the better feedback you'll get. Use the example, effect, coach and commit formula to receive feedback:

- If you don't connect with the feedback, ask for an EXAMPLE.
- If don't understand the importance or impact of your behaviour, ask for the EFFECT.
- If you are unsure how to make changes, ask for some COACHING to set goals and create an action plan.
- If you want help to stay accountable, ask for it through COMMITMENT.

Some of the following questions may help you decide whether it's appropriate for you to ask for feedback. Ask yourself:

1. When was the last time I had a review of my work and my level of productivity? (Perhaps it was so long ago, you don't recall what was discussed.)
2. I don't know what is expected on this task or project. Eg. What are the success factors?
3. Was a specific task or project not completed well?
4. How can I work out the cause of the problems with a project or task?
5. Someone else got a promotion I applied for. I was equally suited for the role. What have I missed or what do I need to do to get that same promotional opportunity?
6. I did a fantastic job completing the task/project and I would like some help identifying how to take it further. How can I replicate the success in other areas?

7. What's happening to my role and what opportunities are available to me given recent changes?
8. I want to stay with this company, yet this role is not right for me. What skills do I need to develop or improve to be considered for other roles?
9. I can't stand working with Bob. He's my colleague but speaks to me and treats me like a subordinate. How do I deal with him?
10. I think I run a tight ship, but the staff satisfaction survey results are low. Productivity seems okay, but staff turnover is creeping up. What can I do to address these issues?

If any of these questions even slightly relate to you, then ask for feedback.

A FINAL NOTE ABOUT FOLLOWING UP

Do it! If you set times and dates in your calendar to follow up, check progress and give ongoing support, then stick to it. The manager who doesn't follow up sends the message that the employee is not worthy or valued. This results in limited, if any, action being implemented.

Helping your people be accountable is a key component of people productivity.

Follow up has been mentioned multiple times in this

book – got the unsubtle hint yet? So many managers and leaders miss out on massive engagement and productivity boosting opportunities simply because they don't schedule the follow up time. Busy consumes their day.

THANK YOU NOTES: PRAISE

Whenever I receive the gift of wisdom and time from someone I know could have been doing something else, I send them a handwritten thank you note.

Some may call it a strategy. I call it good manners. It costs me very little to send a note of thanks.
And sometimes I get a message back, such as, "Oh thank you so much, I didn't expect that. So nice to get something handwritten, something personal."

TAKING BACK TIME!

The dental practice manager had admitted to avoiding a feedback – difficult – conversation for almost a year! Once the conversation structure was in place, the conversation took place the next day.

Following this feedback, performance improved bit by bit. The manager's commitment to follow up ensured steady progress.

The manager calculated that hours had been spent discussing with colleagues and senior leaders the performance issue. Added to this were the hours spent almost fortnightly having conversations with the employee – conversations that circled the issue but didn't make a difference. While the effort was well intended at the time, according to the manager, it really was wasted.

WHAT I KNOW FOR SURE IS...
TIME IS NOT MONEY:
YOU CAN ALWAYS GET MORE
MONEY BUT YOU CAN NEVER
GET MORE TIME.
SPEND IT WISELY!

– SALLY FOLEY-LEWIS

CHAPTER 18

THERE'S ALWAYS MORE

You've made it to the final chapter! But in many ways, this is the beginning. There will always be more to learn, think through, reflect upon, implement and adapt. Your day-to-day will always bring new opportunities, challenges, false starts, seemingly never-ending issues, crises and unexpected (good and not so good) endings. Thinking these things won't happen is naive. Not wishing for them yet being ready and expecting them is smart.

As Ernest Hemingway said, "The world breaks everyone, and afterward, some are strong at the broken places." You've no doubt been through a change in your life that, while it may not have been a pleasant experience, has given you the skills, knowledge and insight to make you a smarter, more resilient person.

The productive leader knows to expect the unexpected without being overwhelmed by that realisation. They plan their actions and strategies to build resilience. The productive leader keeps watch for potential issues without letting the expectation become an excuse for inaction or a trigger for procrastination.

One of my mentors has a great description for this: "A well-planned spontaneous response."

YOU ARE AT A DECISION POINT

Throughout this book, you have read about productive leaders who have made changes. You've read about how much time these leaders have taken back as a result. You'll notice they *took* the time back; it wasn't given to them. To take time back requires effort. While the examples only highlight the time saved based on a singular change, imagine the cumulative effect when productive leaders make the effort to find multiple ways to improve their personal, professional and people productivity.

You're worth the investment. And you'll soon find two hours a day to spend however you would like to spend it: with family, friends, "me time" or finding more ways to build your bottom line.

You can put this book down and slip back into your old, comfortable habits. I wouldn't blame you if you did. Change can be hard work. And while you're not afraid of a bit of hard work, what pulls you back into old habits is the fear of the unknown. If this is you, revisit Chapter 6 on Procrastination.

To get started, it's a good idea to take one chapter, dive back into that topic and make changes that will bring you the best returns. Take the time to reflect on your learning in that chapter or focus area. The following structure will help you:

1. The way I want to demonstrate this skill or area of my productive leadership is …

   _____

   _____

2. If I gave myself a score out of 10 for how good I currently am in this skill or area, it would be …/10.

3. Three top reasons why I give myself this score (why some things aren't working):
   1. _____
   2. _____
   3. _____

4. Now, having revisited the relevant chapter for the skill or focus area I want to improve, the top three actions I will start now are:
   1. _____
   2. _____
   3. _____

5. I'll know I have achieved them or succeeded when (finish this sentence) …

   _____

   _____

6. Sometimes the actions you determine for yourself could be quite significant, possibly overwhelming. If this is the case, what is the first step you will take towards achieving the three actions you stated above?

_____

_____

_____

THE VALUE OF MENTORS

When you hear someone explain how they succeeded in a field or endeavour, most of the time they acknowledge the support, wisdom and experience of a mentor. Never underestimate the value of having a mentor, even for a short while.

You could have a skill-relevant mentor, career mentor or leadership mentor. To excel in productive leadership, look at your network and identify who is great at something you need guidance with. For example, you might know a leader who heads a department in another organisation and is excellent at email and task management.

If this is an area you know you need to improve, ask the leader if they could be your mentor in this specific area. You might be surprised by how honoured they feel because you asked.

For example, in an internal mentoring program for a large national retail firm, the mentees nominated who they would like to be their mentors. When the mentors received the requests, the responses were heart-warming: "Really, I'd love to be a mentor, I'm so thrilled to be asked," and, "I'd be delighted and I'm honoured to be asked." Of about 50 potential mentors, only two declined and one of those was because they were resigning so the timing wasn't right.

If you want more help, then please get in touch with me. I would be delighted to support you through mentoring, delivering team workshops or speaking at your next team meeting.

278 | SALLY FOLEY-LEWIS

WANT MORE?

Sally Foley-Lewis is a productivity and leadership expert. She speaks, mentors and runs workshops to help leaders and dedicated professionals become exceptionally productive and confident leaders.

Sally writes a blog, produces the People and Management podcast, is the creator of the self-coaching resource Management Success Cards®, and her first book was a quick guide to *Successful Feedback*.

To find out about Sally's resources, programs and workshops, go to www.sallyfoleylewis.com. You can also connect with Sally on the following social media platforms:

LINKEDIN
www.linkedin.com/in/sallyfoleylewis/

TWITTER
twitter.com/SallyFoleyLewis

FACEBOOK
www.facebook.com/PeopleAndProductivity/

YOUTUBE
www.youtube.com/user/SallyFoleyLewis

OTHER RESOURCES

SUCCESSFUL FEEDBACK
http://bit.ly/FeedbackBook

MANAGEMENT SUCCESS CARDS®
http://bit.ly/MangtSuccessCards

PEOPLE AND MANAGEMENT PODCAST

iTunes:
http://bit.ly/PeopleMantiTunes

Website:
http://bit.ly/PeopleMantWeb

Stitcher/Android:
http://bit.ly/PeopleMantStitcher

A LEADER HAS A COMPASS
IN THEIR MIND AND A
MAGNET IN THEIR HEART.

– ANONYMOUS

Made in the USA
San Bernardino, CA
29 August 2018